This book has been compiled from the hilarious agricultural ramblings of NFU man and part-time farmer's boy, Mike Sanderson. Many of the stories have been previously published in the NFU's "North West Farmer" magazine or in the "Westmorland Messenger", but are gathered here, in a semblance of disorder for the first time with cartoons by Paul Gurney.

Yows & Cows

A bit of Westmorland Wit

Mike Sanderson

A Hayloft Publication

First published 2000

by Hayloft Publishing,
Great Skerrygill, South Stainmore,
Kirkby Stephen, Cumbria, CA17 4EU.

Tel. 017683 42300 or Fax. 017683 41568
e-mail: icetalk@icetalk.co.uk
website: www.hayloft.org.uk

© 2000 Mike Sanderson

ISBN 0 9523282 0 8

Cover Photograph by Peter Koronka
Design & Production by Hayloft Publishing

Printed & bound by Lintons Printers, Co. Durham.

This book is dedicated to the memory of Rodger Blenkinship.

Between starting to put this together and it going to print, we lost poor Rodger with cancer on the 1st March 2000, at the age of 40. You'll find his words and deeds liberally spread through the pages of this book just as his words and deeds have been liberally spread through our lives in recent years.

He was part of the family and you couldn't ask for a better mate or work mate. I've not got a brother and Rodger is as near as I'm ever likely to get. It just doesn't seem fair such a decent, hard working lad should be taken so young. I'd like to dedicate this to him and hope that when those who knew him read this, they will smile and have pleasant memories of him.

Thanks for help with production of this book go to Paul Gurney, Keith Alderson (for drawing of the dog), Peter Koronka for the photographs and Dawn Robertson for initially encouraging me to write for *The Messenger* and then giving me the courage to go ahead with this.

A Potted History

I began life on 18 October 1955 being born in Brampton near Carlisle. I was christened Michael James Sanderson being named after my grandfathers - Michael Morland Sanderson and Percy James Dewhurst Bishop. As you can see I could have ended up with Percy Morland Sanderson and who knows where I could have ended up with a name like that.

We moved to Hause Farm, Shap, in the February of 1956 and I've been heafed there ever since. I don't remember much about it, but I do remember life before electric, steam engines and bankers on Shap Summit, being transported about in the back of an ex-Post Office van (no car), milk stands and hay sweeps. All now long gone but nostalgia to anyone my age brought up on a hill farm.

I was schooled at Shap Primary School and then Heversham Grammar School and was reaching the end of my schooling without a clue of what I was going to do. I went to the job centre at Penrith in the Easter of 1974 before I took my "A" levels. Those were the days when you chose your employer if you were worth anything, not the other way round as it is nowadays. I wouldn't like to be a youngster looking for a job today never mind a 40 something as I am.

I was dressed like you used to be dressed in 1974. Flared jeans patched with red corduroy, baggy white jumper down to my knees and hair somewhere near my shoulders (those were the days). I said I expected to get four "A" levels and I had an interest in farming. The lady flicked through the cards - no computers in those days - and said there was a vacancy at the NFU Mutual just around the corner. So she rang up and sent me round in my "trendy" attire. I didn't expect to make much of an impression but was promised a job if I got the exams I reckoned I'd get.

I remember getting a letter whilst I was still at school advising me my starting salary had been re-adjusted because of a change in the cost of living index and it had risen to £20 and a few pennies a week. I thought I was made.

I got my exams as promised and started life as a management trainee and was quite happy for several years. I was also helping out on the farm. By 1979 I was sick of shuffling pieces of paper about and left to work at home.

John Lancaster and Ron Mellor who ran the NFU office at Kendal heard of my plans and offered me part-time work in their office. This was ideal and worked well as Hause Farm has only ever really been a one and a half man farm. I spent over ten happy years at Kendal - three days a week working among the farmers down there who called byres shippons, fertiliser till and thought I spoke with a funny accent. It's amazing the difference that few miles over Shap Fell makes.

I stayed there until 1990 when the vacancy came up for the NFU post at Appleby and, as a 34-year-old with a young family and no job security I had to decide which way to jump.

I jumped for the full time NFU posting at Appleby and having a grounding in farming and insurance matters was lucky enough to get it. As I said earlier, I'm still heafed at Shap. Full time doesn't include every night and weekend and I am allowed some holiday so I can still fit in quite a bit of farming. Keeping my hand in on the practical side helps no end when dealing with farmers and their problems (and trying to keep father's paperwork straight).

Father, although 70, runs 650 Cheviot/Rough yows with Cheviot becoming more and more predominant and still has a few cattle, eighteen or twenty at the last count so you can see we have our hands full, specially at busy times such as lambing/clipping/dipping/haytiming and the like.

A description of the farm would not be complete without mention of Rodger Blenkinship who helps at weekends and busy times and is part of the family.

My own family are wife Marian, daughter Jane who I usually refer to as Can-R-Cum, as you cannot get away without her and son James who is football daft, or more precisely Newcastle United daft.

Hill Farmer Spotting

Farmers are good to spot in their working garb with tatty old jackets, lots of clart and an odour of silage, slurry and the like, they are bad to miss.

Get them all washed and scrubbed and it can prove more interesting. The odour factor can still come into play if in a warm enclosed space for any length of time.

A ruddy complexion is also a good guide especially when it stops half way up the forehead exposing that part that lives under a cap or woolly hat for 90 per cent of its life.

Hands are a give away as well - usually outsized, generally mucky, often with chunks knocked out where the spanner slipped or a finger or two got nipped when they were somewhere they shouldn't really have been.

The tweed jacket and farmerish head gear are easy to distinguish but

on a trip to London recently it was even easier than that - they were the only ones who spoke back to you. How can someone on the tube with his face within six inches of yours refuse to admit you exist? They're strange folk down there.

Farmers on the road are not just as easy to sort out as they were, due to all these new age 4x4ers. Mind clarts are a dead give away again as the vast majority of these new converts to 4 wheel drive trucks never go anywhere near any muck, and if they did, their pride and joy would be washed and polished within 24 hours.

Neither do they meander down the middle of the road minding everybody's business but their own checking on Jack next door's poor crop of grass and his sheep that need worming.

There's another clue to sorting farmers. Having played quite a bit of rugby I can confirm they are usually quite useful and nearly always as hard as they come. Well, if you can handle and geld a ten-month-old Limmy bullock some so called hard case is not going to prove too much of a problem.

When stripped out the vital clue is the back of the calf muscle. If there's a dark looking band with no hair, he's definitely a farmer. That's where his wellies have been rubbing.

Hill Sheep

Auction Sceptics

Tup lowsing is the beginning of the farming calender for the local hill farmers. Putting the yows to the tups sounds very simple but, first you've got to get your tups.

Mid-October in Kirkby sees three days of Swaledale tup sales. These are the three days when hill farmers probably do themselves the biggest dis-service on the publicity front. The public at large read headlines of £20,000 or £30,000 being paid for an animal and think they all make that or thereabouts.

The mart reports in the papers don't carry news of black tup lambs weighing 30 kilos only making £12. They're a bit guilty of only passing on the good news.

I often think when watching tup sales (or any others for that matter, it's just there's more folk there) it must be an awful job for the uninitiated to get into. It must be intimidating having the confidence in your own judgement in front of hundreds of sceptics (sorry farmers).

On top of that you have to make sense of what the auctioneer is saying and probably most important of all to be sure you're not bidding against yourself!

Then, when you've got your tups bought there's still the matter of "luck" which is far too complicated to go into here.

At the Tup Sale

I got a late invitation to attend the big Swaledale Tup Sales at Kirkby Stephen to provide insurance cover on the tups. Not only was this a welcome source of extra business, but a thoroughly enjoyable couple of afternoons and evenings.

I was allotted a corner of a desk in the mart office in among the 'office girls'. Things started well as one of them immediately started shedding her clothes. I don't usually have this effect on women! In reality it was just her jumper and it was because it was warm.

Everyone was offered insurance when they came to pay for their tups and I looked after them if they did. I had a from to fill in which was reasonably straight forward, but the question which raised most comment was: 'Had they ever been bankrupt?'.   Most of the replies were pretty unrepeatable, but the general consensus was - not yet but not far off!

All the farmers have a different view of insurance; some were mad keen to insure tups at a relatively modest price and some were quite happy to take the risk on tups worth several thousands of pounds, looking on it as an ordinary day to day risk of farming.

My favourite moment was when a price was given on quite a dear tup, but the farmer said he had never insured one before and didn't think he'd start now. As he left the office I wished him luck. He must have just about got out on the street, then turned on his heels and came back. He'd changed his mind and he blamed me - if I hadn't wished him good luck he wouldn't have thought about it again!

Another nice moment was when someone landed in the office wanting to know where he could find the tup he had just bought. Tongue firmly in cheek, I told him it would have a black face with a white nose end - with that description he thought it might take him a bit to find it.

The moment of highest tension over the whole two days was with about an hour of selling to go on the second day, when the computer went down and froze. For a number of minutes (which seemed like hours) no bills were produced or cheques issued while phone calls were made and computer keys punched. Fortunately the systems fired back into life and the bustle and hurley burley in the mart office set off again.

You didn't see a lot of 'trade' in the office, but they had been a good couple of days with prices up, I understand, about the £10,000 mark. I suppose whether it's good or not depends on if you're a buyer or a seller! It seems strange that prices are up when times are hard, but going for quality is one way of dealing with the crisis.

I should close by thanking Stuart Bell for his invitation and all his ladies for all their help.

In the Dark

I was standing having a pee in the loo at Kirkby Mart when I was joined by one of my more elderly clients. "By it's dark in here," he says.

"It's a bad job if you can't find him in the dark," I replied.

"Find him in the dark? I can't find him it in the daylight," he says!

Tup lowsing

I take a day or two off in November to help get ready for tupping. We had eventually got finished and were sitting having our teas with all yows dipped, tailed, dosed and divided into various lots and tups 'lowsed.'

Mother said: "You'll have some happy gentlemen out there."

"Yes," said Father, "and lots of happy ladies."

On the subject of tailing sheep, one of my favourite stories is of the local farm lass who crammed the pen full of sheep to tail the yows, tailed and tailed away forgetting the tups were also in the pen.

When she had finished, she had done a grand job but the tups, much to the locals' amusement were tailed as well. Sexual equality for sheep I suppose - cold backsides for tups and yows alike.

The Pen Man

I bought my NFU pens at the end of October and was amused when the sales rep. asked if I could explain why he had seen lots of sheep round about with their tails clipped like poodles. I explained in graphic detail (much to Tina's amusement).

Fitness training for hoggs

We had about twenty lambs left at Christmas we didn't know what to do with. They weren't fit to sell so they just ran about with the yows and got a bit of feed. They looked to be doing a bit of good so father sorted them off and fed them a bit harder.

They were in a field he went past on his way to just about every batch of sheep he fed and they spent all day chasing round and round the field after him. Then they even got to laking like week old lambs.

He thought they were running off any feed they were eating but he was pleasantly surprised when we got them in just before lambing. He was off to Kirkby with them and they'd averaged £30, which was £20 to £25 more than they were worth at Christmas. He wouldn't have won the gurning prize that Tuesday night. In fact, I am sure there was the start of a smile in the corner of his mouth - No - I must have been mistaken!

Mistaken Identity

Most of you will have done it but not many own up to it - kept a wether hogg thinking it was a gimmer. We find we have got to be especially careful now keeping Cheviots as Rough Fell wethers were always better to spot by their horns.

Well we failed to spot one wether but worse than that he got kept as a shearling. As you can imagine, he didn't take the tup but the second time he was clipped he was covered in marking so we couldn't fail to spot him. He didn't get put to the tup this back end as he is in my deep freeze - and by he is good.

Names for sheep

Cheviot sheep often have a bit of black on them which can help with easy recognition and a good name:

Black ear - Black lug (not very original)

Black leg - Arthur (Scargill)

Black patch on eye - Pugwash

Black patch on back - Saddleback

Black all over - TINO (named after Faustino Asprilla Newcastle's Colombian centre forward)

Black.... you know - when you're not allowed into a secret society.

Brought down to Earth

A couple of months ago, we got our sheep scanned for the first time. What a boon. The scanning man was 100% spot on. It really did make life a lot easier as we seem to get more twins each year. We thought we'd caught him out a couple of times, but it was the shedding man's fault (father), saying that he blamed the smitting man (me) - not enough marking!

Last back-end we had our yows ready to put to the tups, tailed, sorted, dosed, etc. but father said was too early to lowse them as they would start lambing on the 10th. When I pointed out the 10th April was Good Friday and he'd be fully staffed then he changed his mind and away they went. So you'll have no trouble guessing what I'm busy with at present. We scanned for the first time last year and have repeated the exercise this time as lambing went so much easier. I wrote about it last year and Adrian played war with me because I didn't give him a mention, well he got his mention so he'd better be as accurate as last year - 100 per cent or he'll be getting another mention! We weren't quite as new-fangled with the job this year and saved a shilling or two by not scanning the tups!

The third year we scanned and we expected Adrian to be up to his usual standard. I'll always remember father's reaction after his first visit. After two hours, we'd about 500 sheep scanned and Adrian had never shut up all the way through. "What a waste of money, what can he tell, he can't have been concentrating, he's never stopped talking." Well he likely must have been concentrating because the job was spot on.

The worst thing about Adrian's system is his fancy computer printout. I was busy telling father what our lambing percentage was and how many lambs we had prior to lambing last year when I was told in no uncertain terms to put the bit of paper in the fire. Father is no great believer in percentages, the only number of lambs that matter are the number you either unload at the auction or keep as gimmer hoggs. The rest doesn't bear thinking about. When everyone else is talking about pence per kilogram, he points out it's pounds per lamb that really matter. That's hill farmers logic for you.

I visited Adrian about a week or ten days after he'd got through his main scanning period. He'd been busy getting all the information on computer and his bills sent out and I don't think he'd really got a look outside.

We were busy discussing insurance matters when he told us he was going to stop farming and start to sell insurance. His wife (whom I suspect does most of the work in any case) said: "Adrian you haven't started farming yet."

Into the Valley of Death

The month of March can be most frustrating for the poor old hill farmer. The time between getting out the cake-bag and starting to lamb, or after if you keep feeding them. At the start your old yows are as sensible as old yows get, but day by day they get dafter and dafter until you can't make a thing to them.

Yows to the left of you, yows to the right of you, yows in front of you blethering and running. How many of you have been flat across the field, ahead of a hundred crazy yows with the bag when you get the dreaded horn down the wellie, over you go, end over whatsit, to be trampled underfoot.

I can remember landing on top of an old yow. She didn't regard herself as unlucky - she had her head in the bag eating cake for all she was worth with my considerable frame on top of her.

Can some of the older experienced sheep men out there explain why they either want the last piece of cake in the bag or the bit in mid-air between the bag and the ground. Beats me!

When you go to the fell, they remind me of Red Indians in the old cowboy films, standing on the hill tops, waiting to swoop down on you. They don't always get it right though. We have seen some amazed motorists who pull off the M6 for a rest or a thermos and park up on the fell and find their vehicle surround with yows twenty deep.

We have all tried to outsmart them - going at a different time or through a different gate, using a decoy, getting someone to go in the opposite direction with an empty bag before you make a break for it. However inventive you are, it never seems to work for long.

My father is breeding out of Rough Fells into Cheviots and this only makes things worse. They're half as fast and half as daft again. He buys his tups at Lockerbie and I'm sure the only ones he considers are those that come into the ring at 25mph and hit the opposite side flat out.

Father's new strain of sheep are called North Country Fuel Injected Turbo Charged GT Cheviots. They take a bit of keeping up with and he is going to have to patent a new eight foot shepherd's stick and a bike with another gear to go with them.

It makes for sport in lambing time when you lamb outside in fields no less than six acres (2.429 hectares in MAFF speak). But that's another story.

People often look on sheep as being stupid, but there's one thing for sure you cannot question, and that's their memories. Father got his first delivery of cake for the year and went to the fell with his snacker. It had not seen light of day for ten months but the old girls hadn't forgotten it. Instead of heading in the opposite direction because he might have the dog on board, they met him flat out and were straight round the back where the cake comes out.

Mind, when you think about it, they never forget the smell of dipping. One sniff and they dig their toes in for all they're worth. I can remember trying to put yows up a ramp on to a clipping trailer. The last time they had gone up a ramp it was on to a mobile dipper and they would have none of it.

April 1996

Lambing time can be the most satisfying time of year on a hill farm. We lamb outside and on a warm, sunny, spring day when things are going well, there isn't a better job. When there's a bite of grass and the yows have plenty of milk and their maternal instincts are working to there full potential it's marvellous, nature at its best. You help with leg back here and a bit of sorting out there and the job goes on wonderfully well.

Then, of course, as we all know, you have just been lulled into a false sense of security. The wind turns into the east, the temperature drops three degrees and instead of the sun on your back, you can hardly look into the wind for hail biting into your face.

The land which was just beginning to have a green look about it, turns a grey colour and the maternal instincts disappear altogether and half the flock seem to produce offspring they want to disown immediately.

You have to discard the boots and instead of trousers and T-shirt you put back on your wellies, leggings, holey coat and woolly hat.

It's amazing how many times it happens like this at this time of year. I am writing this in mid-April when everything is going reasonably well, but you'd be surprised how many people have reminded me of the lambing of 1981 when the weather was exceptionally good until it came a foot of snow in a day at the end of April and a lot of sheep were lost.

They are a happy lot, farmers. The other observation goes a bit like this: "By, there's a lot of lambs about this year. By, with the weather being so good, folk are having good lambings. By, lambs'll be worth nowt at back end!' - some folk are never happy.

One of my favourite lambing tales is about a local farmer who was a big, big, man. You talk about hands like shovels but his clenched fist looked like a turnip. His neighbour reckoned to be very worried about the condition of his yows. He said: "They're getting weaker by the day. They can't hang on much longer."

"What's wrong, are they short of something?" The reply was: "No, they daren't lie down to sleep or he lambs them!"

Oscar

This year's lamb trade has been a revelation and in particular, light lambs on a Tuesday night at Kirkby. I understand one hill farmer from Shap is on the short list for an academy award. He was in the ring selling Rough wether lambs for an excellent price looking as miserable as sin. You would swear the dealers had just begged his last halfpenny off him. He reckons its policy never to look too pleased but, there's a limit. Mind, this is the man who when he says his trade was OK has had an absolute flier. No prizes for guessing his identity.

April 1997

I am writing this just before I take my annual week's holiday to help my father lamb his yows at Shap.

For about a month I will devote every morning, evening and day away from the NFU striving to keep as many lambs as possible alive. Every sheep farmer in this area is in exactly the same position, or even worse. At least at Shap when it gets dark we retire for the day - father has no sheep shed.

Bearing this in mind, I am sure it makes all those sheep farmers as angry as me when you see on the television and in the media the preachings by the animal welfare/green wellie brigade about lamb fatalities.

I wonder what they think would happen if nature were allowed to take its course? I am sure a lot of you are like me, Henry Brewis enthusiasts, and smile at his pictures of yows laid out having fulfiled this life's ambition of having all legs pointing skywards and his description of his all purpose lambing tool - a spade!

But in all seriousness, it is in every farmer's interest to do his utmost to keep his stock in as good a condition and as comfortable as possible, not only is it his second nature to care for his stock to the best of his ability, it also makes sound economic sense.

I think farmers as a whole should be proud of the job they do and not be shy in saying so. How many other walks of life can boast the levels of time, care and devotion the farming industry can? Given the levels of financial investment there's no sin in making a profit either.

April 1998

The lambing time fun started early for me when, with Mam and Dad having a weekend off a couple of weeks before we started to lamb, leaving me in charge.

I just had the sheep to feed and keep an eye on everything. I arrived on Saturday morning and the yow that might need another shot of calcium before she recovered was laid stone dead. The first lot of sheep I went to feed produced a yow with a dead lamb and I had another with a slipped lamb when I went to the fell.

As a result, I spent Saturday hunting for a couple of pet lambs, skinning the casualties and mothering-on. Sunday brought an improvement but still had a yow with a prolapse to deal with. Talk about Sod's Law.

Father returned and couldn't really tell me off too much as none of the carnage was really my fault. He did point out I'd paid too much for my pet lambs though. It went through my mind what could have gone wrong. I could have bent his pick-up, had his bike stolen or lost a cow but nothing would be too bad unless something happened to the dog. If he'd got hurt or hit on the road, I'd have to go into hiding.

Lambing came on Good Friday with the Easter weekend and taking a week off work I had thirteen of the first seventeen days at home, it all worked out quite well.

April 1999

At this time of year I like to put a few notes together about one or two amusing things that have gone on at lambing time. This year, I don't think anyone would print the words to describe the carry on we've had.

Last month I said I was hoping for some good weather for my holidays - and what happened - Arctic weather followed by monsoon conditions. I detest wearing leggings but we were into the third week of lambing before I dared venture out of the house without them on. I'm not too keen on hats either but wear a woolly hat to compensate for my lack of thatch. Well, that was no good and I took to wearing father's "Deputy Dawg" - you know the ones with the flaps that fasten under your chin.

I can distinctly remember one particular morning about 7am standing with Rodger over our umpteenth disaster of the morning with water running off the peak of the "Deputy" like a tap. Most of what Rodger said was unrepeatable but basically he was ready for early retirement.

In lambing time, I often catch out Rodger, especially if he's got daughter Jane, better known as Can-R-Cum, in the motorbike trailer with him. Go quietly through some right sticky puddle till you can't see the treads on the wheels then open it out on a bit of decent going and cover the pair of them in puddle.   Mind, this wasn't really the year for testing anyone's sense of humour, patience was getting paper thin.

There wasn't much to amuse us but an article in the "Westmorland Gazette" on lambing at Raisgill Hall came close to it and I quote: "The birth of lambs such as the woolly teddy bears resulting from a new cross between North Country Cheviots and Rough Fells heralds the start of a new year for farmer Mr. Dunning."

"Huh - a new cross," said father, "we've been chasing the bloody things for the last 30 years." We lamb a lot of them and Rodger calls them all sorts of things but I've yet to hear him use woolly teddy bears. It's certainly not what I called the old yow who got among my feet and tipped me over into the wall. I cracked my head on a through and I needed six stitches in my head.

I bled like a stuck pig and father took me to hospital but said I had to go in the pick-up as I was bleeding too much to get into the car. However, I was allowed to sit on the dog's seat in the front. I thought my days of sitting in Penrith Hospital on a Saturday afternoon getting my head sown up were long gone. The doctor who sewed me up was a bit of a card and I told him to put plenty of stitches in so I'd get a bit of sympathy. All my wife Marian said was she was pleased she'd washed all my smelly farming clothes and underwear the day before!

We turned the geld yows back to the fell and Rodger thought one was a lamber as he couldn't see a smit on it. I said it was going as if it was geld. "They all go as if they're geld," he said - and he's right. We all get a year older every year, our dog included, and he's either eleven or twelve. We thought he mightn't manage but after a couple of days he got fittened up, limbered up, his patience wore thin and his temper went and the job was a good un. Just like the Mounties, we always got our yow.

Rodger has been away for six months in New Zealand and has been taking comic lessons. he threw his woolly hat in the front of the pick-up and said: "What do you call that?.....CHUCK BERRY." Oh very good. Not bad for straight off the top of my head!

Blethering Yow

One of our haulier/farmers from Greenholme had a good lambing tale. One of his old yows had lost a twin lamb and she'd hung around some rabbit holes blethering away. He looked and did a bit of digging but couldn't find anything but the old yow would not give up.

He comes back and digs and digs and digs and digs and eventually rescues the twin lamb - what a wonderful victory. He'd saved the lamb from its ultimate aim - to die as young as possible. Then what happens? A day or two later, the damned lamb goes and dies on him. To put it in football terms, it won the return leg on away goals!

Pet lamb competition

I have a competition for you - guess the name of my mother's pet lamb? If you need a clue or two he's a peroxide blonde Cheviot tup lamb who drinks as much as he can and cries a lot - see bottom of page for answer.

Costa del Shap

At the beginning of May I was complemented on my tan and asked where I'd been on my holidays. I'm afraid it had very little to do with the sun and everything to do with frost, wind and rain. It's what you get on the Costa del Shap at the height of the season (lambing season that is).

I must be getting old. This last month I've spent my time running between lambs and IACS forms and, after a meal, can sleep at the drop of a hat. I was amused by a local farmer's wife who was telling me her husband had a leg up and she was doing the bullocking and they were busy lambing and she was that tired she could sleep on the clothes line.

That's right - Gazza. Father says when he's drunk all his milk if he makes £35 he will have only lost £25.

Just as well it was a leg up and not over!

After the mildest of winters, lambing time came hand in hand with Jack Frost and a whole host of brass monkeys for the first frosty week of the year. It was then followed by about the wettest week. This was after mowing the lawn at Shap in March on the 1000 foot contour! I know what you're thinking - why didn't we just turn a couple of old yows in - we wouldn't dare! The lambing men took worse with the weather than the lambs as I don't think we lost one to the elements - they found much better excuses.

We seem to get more twins each year and have taken to numbering them. We often get them in for the first night and Rodger and I number them as we put them out. Occasionally you get lost with them and we ended up with two sets of No. 36s and a 49 and a 49A. Father played war when he looked at them so we had one set with pictures of a little man on to keep him going.

Post Natal Depression

Lambs don't follow too well after they've been in and will follow anything bar their mother. How they can think you, the pick-up or the bike are their mother, I fail to gather. I may get to smelling like an old yow but I don't look like one.

On our rounds we came across a new dropped lamb with its mother about ten yards away looking in the opposite direction doing its best to ignore it. I said to Rodger I thought it was a case of Post Natal Depression. We'd had a savage day or two and he thought he might be suffering from it too.

The most amusing part of lambing time was mother's pet lamb, a wreckling triplet. If you imagine a head on a half-pint glass with four Bic biros for legs, you've got it. What an article. My kids got their hands on it so it was saved the Hause Farm head butt. Our post-lady used to play with it and it became quite a talking point. Its daily progress had to be reported to the staff in the Co-op at Shap. It lived in a box by the Aga for a fortnight and, when let out for exercise, mothered itself on to the pet dog. It was a sight sat curled up with the dog or trailing around the garth after it. It did eventually get mothered on to a ewe and the latest news is it can still walk under her belly without touching her.

We've all had to put up with weeks of electioneering which is of very little entertainment value, but I did hear one of the political commentators say interviewing politicians is akin to nailing custard to the wall, which I thought was a good one. But, as Rodger pointed out, after polishing off his steam pudding, he hasn't come across my mother's custard.

Pet Lambs

On the whole, we had a good lambing but did have a bad patch when we needed a few pet lambs. We got one off my Uncle Brian who swore blind it had come straight off a yow. Father was convinced it hadn't seen a yow for a fortnight. He battled with it for ages before he persuaded it yows and not bottles were the best source of milk.

We had another which, previous to its life with us, had been numbered as a twin in one colour and smit for various reasons with two other colours. The old yow we mothered it on to didn't half look when the white skin was removed to reveal a multi-coloured lamb. I was sent off to get two pet lambs and expected an awful telling off when I landed back with five. All manner of catastrophes seemed around every corner and within three days they were all mothered on and accepted.

As usual, we had some fun catching father's Turbo Charged Cheviots, most of them with a bit of guile and cunning you can dab whilst their maternal instincts still get the better of them, but a few others, which Rodger christened sporting models, prick their ears and tails up as you enter the field and then it's just a matter of hot pursuit.

The best chase ended with Rodger, me and the yow in a heap on the ground with mission accomplished but a right angle bend in Rodger's brand new aluminium stick just purchased by father at great expense. I had the misfortune to break my right hand catching one. I didn't go to the doctor as I've done it before playing rugby but Lesley the vet confirmed my diagnosis. Fortunately, it was not my pen driving hand so it didn't slow the stream of IACS forms.

As we lamb outside, Rodger and I tend to do the field work and leave father with the inside work in the casualty department. We spent a great deal of time with a yow with twins that had a bad lambing. The lambs had been badly nipped and struggled to foot and suck. We did persevere but they were very slow and we eventually came back in to find their skins on two pet lambs. Father swore blind they had head-butted a metal pillar in the barn.

While having our coffee during a break in the proceedings, Rodger was studying the situations vacant in the "Herald" and thought he could manage a job as a midwife. Quite what the expectant mother would make of him rolling up his sleeves, catching and upending her in a corner of the delivery room, I don't know. His delivery method may leave a little to be desired, especially if she had a leg back. The proud father needn't be too pleased either if Rodger pulled a can of fluorescent orange spray from his pocket and proceeded to paint a large number 14 on the side of mother and child. Father would take the right ones home though!

Rodger

When the weather's bad we tend to house all the twins and delicate looking cases that lamb say, after about tea time. Also if you lamb a Cheviot
shearling you don't let it off to see if it mothers. You bring it in and make
sure it mothers. Catching it once is bad enough, catching it twice is silly.
One evening we had all the old byres and boxes full and the Dutch barn
split into pens and father playing war as we had over 40 cases in his care.

Can-R-Cum is only eleven but nothing phases her and she can handle
all the blood and gore part, from a dog who takes great delight in eating
cleansings and yows who eat their own cleansings. "That's disgusting,"
was her favourite phrase but it didn't keep her away. Rodger and I were
working among sheep by the A6 near Shap one morning when I com-
mented how quiet the road was. "Well" he explained, "It's only 8
o'clock. It's a Bank Holiday Monday and not everyone is as daft as us."
Sort of sums up farming, doesn't it!

Even when I'm at work I go through to Shap for the morning and
night shifts, but when we got sorted out down to 50 lambers in one field
I skipped the morning shift. My first lie in for almost a month and what
do you think happened? An enormous Tom cat out the back struck up at
about 5.30am making the most awful row and I had my worst night's
sleep all lambing time.

Sure sign of madness

Have you ever talked to a lamb while you're trying to suckle it? You do
it and I don't know why, because they don't listen. It usually goes something like this:

- Come on little lamb let's get you a drink
- Get this in your tummy, it'll get you going
- Don't be silly you've got to drink
- Come on, if you don't suck you'll not live
- You stupid little beggar
- Are you trying to make me angry?
- If you don't suck soon, it will be the end of you
- You stupid so and so - I could break your neck!
AND THEN THE ULTIMATUM
- If you don't square yourself up soon there'll be a pet lamb wearing
your skin

The tail of the black sheep

We had a cross Texel/Jacob ewe that produced one black gimmer lamb, licked and mothered it up grand, then a white lamb, licked and mothered it up and immediately refused to have anything further to do with the black lamb.

Try as we may we could not beat her so "Tina Turner" as she became, was confined to the pet lamb pen with "Rod Stewart" a Cheviot tup lamb. The story has a happy ending though, as Tina did go away with a new mother. Mind you, not so happy for the lamb whose skin and mother it inherited.

Can-R-Cum, became the proud owner of Tina Turner. It's one part Jacob, three parts Texel and her grandfather gave it to her for helping. Last year it lambed as a shearling and had a black gimmer which she also got to keep. It's called Tessa - Tessa Sanderson - get it, javelin thrower!

This year it was scanned in lamb with twins which was grand, but then Granda told Jane that Tommy Texel had done the business on the third day of tupping time which logically means Tina Turner was going to lamb on the third day of lambing time.

Monday, 10 April was the official start according to father's calculations making Wednesday the due date. Well Monday passed without too much trouble but the question was still asked: "Has my sheep had her lambs?" Tuesday was a busy day for me on the farm, first thing among the sheep, back to Appleby for nine to my NFUing, ending up at the auction at Kirkby and then back to the farm for the last time round. I'm Chairman of Selectors at Penrith Rugby Club so it was into the Rugby Club for the meeting and it was well after ten when I came through the front door. A little voice came from upstairs: "Has my sheep had her lambs yet?" "No she hasn't, and it's time you were asleep."

This went on all week and the questioning got a bit desperate. It was worse than waiting for Father Christmas to come. The field we lamb the twins in is next to the farmhouse and the blooming old black sheep must have been the best looked lambing sheep in Cumbria.

There was many a time she'd lambed and it turned out to be a lighter coloured stone in the wall behind her or a piece of paper. She made a habit of going and lying behind the wall just to have us on. Well, Wednesday, Thursday and Friday passed without any progress and poor Can-R-Cum was about passed herself. She was with us on the Saturday night and Tina Turner was beginning to think about lambing.

She was behind the wall walking round and round in circles, lying down and getting up and trying to look at her own backside, sniffing the ground and generally preparing herself. She had that guilty look on her face and was looking "sheepish" so the omens were good for Sunday morning.

Poor old Can-R-Cum couldn't cum on Sunday morning because she was playing in a hockey tournament. She was going to have me ringing up at 6.30am out of the lambing field with a progress report on the mobile phone which wouldn't have pleased her mother who enjoys her Sunday lie-ins. We came to a compromise. I would ring at breakfast time.

Fortunately everything had gone well and she had produced two black tup lambs. We told father they were gimmers just to wind him up as he thought he'd be expected to keep them. They'd both sucked so you would have thought that was the last of our troubles with the black yow, but no. She often only had one with her and whenever we mothered them up she wouldn't let them suck. They seemed to be full enough though. When we watched from further off, she often moved on every time they tried to suck, but both lambs were doing well and we finally came to the conclusion they were always at her so she only let them feed when she wanted them to.

As all Jane's sheep have names there was the problem of what to call them. There were several suggestion but I came up with Dwight and Andy (Yorke and Cole of Manchester United). James thought this was dreadful as he is a staunch Newcastle supporter but when I explained they would shortly have their tails and other unmentionable parts of their bodies done away with and hopefully in due course would be made into lamb chops he was quite happy. I am pleased to report mother and two sons progressed well.

Clipping 1997

Although we've well over 800 sheep to clip and have had the clippers in in the past, we managed ourselves by working at nights and weekends with the help of Rodger, which was no mean feat.

Father and Rodger clipped and I was catcher/doser/tipper upper/marker/wrapper/packer. We didn't do so bad for one man, an old man and an office boy but, such is the nature of farming you don't have long to dwell on your achievements before you've got to start sowing a bit of manure, spaining and grading lambs, doing a bit of walling, tidying up a few thistles, etc, etc.....

Another way to go

Sheep can find many ways of dying and I've heard of it before but until this year never seen a sheep pass on whilst being clipped.

Rodger was clipping her and she was only a young sheep. She was a shearling prior to death, a one and half shear when she expired and a two shear by the time we realised her fate.

We weren't sure what the cause of death was, perhaps a twisted gut or heart failure, perhaps even fright but the result was the same.

Clipping 1998

July has been a busy month when we've both haytimed and clipped. With father and Rodger clipping the crack is always good but Rodger was a bit insulted when I marked a yow he'd clipped and said: "There you go Tufty." Don't worry, he got his own back when I was allowed to clip one or two. I wasn't allowed to clip so many, but any that looked roughly clipped were put down to me.

Father was clipping a particularly uneasy old girl and, when he was finished, said: "I'll show you, you old so and so," or words to that effect, and put a large red mark in the middle of her back. We thought that was a bit harsh for kicking a bit, as the mark meant that, come back end, she would grace someone's table. But he did then explain that she was blind on one quarter.

Most of them have been pretty good clipping, but one particularly poor yow was dreadfully sticky. Rodger persevered and got the wool of, but she looked as if she'd been rough plucked. Father refused to let us turn her back to the fell as she'd be sure to stand on the road side and shame him. When she got her lamb mothered up, you could see why she wasn't thriving too well. Her lamb was as big as she was. It also proved lambs identify their mothers by sound, as it would not have recognised her by sight - for sure!

The summer of 1998 was wet. It couldn't stay fine for a whole day if it's life depended on it. We have struggled on among it and got clipped, but we wouldn't have managed that if we hadn't a decent shed to hold the old yows in once they were dry. After almost every clipping session, we have felt sorry for our victims knowing we have sent them out on a bad night without their jackets rather than thinking what a relief it must be in the sweltering heat.

Clipping 1999

It's quite a coincidence that both 1999 and 1998 we finished lambing on the same day as we started clipping. As usual we'll no doubt have a few "geld lambers" to come yet. We've got the tups done and are now among the hoggs and geld yows. Father and Rodger clip and I'm the catcher, doser, wrapper, packer, tar boy, etc. Father's not keen on clipping hoggs so likes to get all the yows. There were two in one pen and he said Rodger could have the one that looked a right tight sticky old git. Rodger got a start and was amused as she wasn't bad going at all and father's yow had hardly any rise, wouldn't sit still and didn't half make him sweat and swear. The most amusing part was it was all his own fault - it's usually the catcher's fault if yows are bad to clip or have mucky backsides.

Father finished clipping a yow, switched off his machine and it almost got off on him. He was rolling about on the floor hanging on to it for grim death. We soon took it off him and marked it. We were giggling at him and asking him what he was on with. Rodger reckoned he didn't know, but it looked illegal.

It's all very well giggling about clipping but we are in a poor hold when the Wool Board are advising farmers to do their own clipping as the wool's worth nowt. I always thought it was the Wool MARKETING Board.

Woollen Woe

There have been many tales of woe over wool cheques but poor uncle Brian's was the best. They clipped about 110 around home and got someone in to clip 54 away from home which cost him £27. His wool cheque duly arrived for £28 leaving him with one pound for all his own work. How does that stack up against the minimum wage?

Father always reckoned the wool cheque should pay your rent so Lord

Lonsdale could be in for a disappointment. Mind I don't think you can send wool by direct debit!

Dip-lomacy

Father had a couple of ladies from the Environment Agency to inspect his dipping facilities last year as there had been some local instances of river and beck pollution.

They landed and explained there had been local pollution in the River Lowther. He took great pleasure in pointing out Hause Farm actually drained south into the Lune and any water would be going in the opposite direction to the Lowther.

Not to be put off, they still carried on and inspected his dipping tub. Well, when he moved to Hause Farm 43 years ago it was relatively modern but time has moved on since then. Where was the plug hole they wanted to know.

Father informed them he'd been looking for it for 40 years and failed to find it so they were quite welcome to have a look as well. They satisfied themselves the sheep weren't wading through a beck once they'd been dipped and much to our surprise went away more or less satisfied. We had expected the worst.

You hear all the old farmers on about when they dipped sheep in DDT and there were never any problems. Well, it's all changed and DDT now stands for Daft Dip Testing!

Dip-loma

When the dipping regulations came in several years ago, father jumped the gun and invested in a 45 gallon drum of dip so had no exam to take for a while. Eventually, of course, the dip got used up and to buy dip someone had to hold a certificate of competence.

As the old saying goes: "You can't teach old dogs new tricks" so I had the exam to take. I'm pleased to say I passed with flying colours, but I had two fair incentives. Firstly, the NFU man would feel a right pillock if it got out he had failed and secondly, I didn't fancy the thought of telling father he had to stump up £50 for a re-test.

They didn't ask any questions about grovelling about on your hands and knees in the draining pen, clearing the drains or filling your wellies full of dipping, standing on a tup's head trying to get him under when he had his feet wedged on one side of the tub and his back on the other.

I do remember the bit about not stressing the sheep by overcrowding the pens. When old yows get a sniff of dip two yows in the catching pen is a crowd and it's only the dipping men who get stressed.

I hope you received your NFU "OP" leaflet and read it carefully. I was reading the list of symptoms, some of which are headaches, loss of co-ordination, diarrhoea, blurred vision, mental confusion, dizziness, nausea and memory loss and I must admit I've learned something - I never realised they used it in beer.

We got the dip bought with this fancy certificate and arranged our dipping weekend for the end of October. Father's haytime men had had a thin do in summer so thankfully, were quite keen to come dipping. We planned it for that really wet Saturday and it was a complete wash-out (literally) so we only had Sunday.

"Monkey" Wearmouth landed first and hadn't been able to find his leggings. Father quickly surrendered his when asked just how close he intended to get to the dipper.

Bob Mason completed the team and the three of us got a start to dip the inside yows. We're quite lucky as the farm's in the middle of our fell and father kept gathering it in bits and kept us going all day.

They're a couple of good workers. Monkey's OK as long as you keep him in bottles of squash. I can understand a man drinking pop mewing bales but, dipping sheep? Bob was OK as we dipped the bigger yows before dinner so he could eat extra helpings of steam pudding and they didn't get him down after dinner.

Our dipping system is pretty modern, or it was when we moved to Hause Farm 43 years ago, so we did well to keep up, dipping 800 sheep in the day.

I've taken my exam and read all the instructions and, bearing this in mind, you would think dip was second only to nuclear waste in the contamination stakes. And, after all that, you get it in a drum it is impossible to pour out of without slattering. With all the who-ha that's gone on over O.P. poisioning, that dip drum was really a disgrace.

Father's old dip was what I would call real dip. It looked and smelt like dip. This stuff looked and smelt like paint stripper. His first remark when he landed back after we had started was: "What are you dipping these sheep in, diesel?"

Retirement

I get asked on numerous occasions: "When is the old man giving up?"
He's now rising 71. I wouldn't dare ask him, but the best I can tell you
is we ran out of coloured tags for our gimmer lambs so we set him off to
buy some more and he landed back with plenty for another three years
and didn't know if he'd got enough.

Allergic reaction

Different people get affected in different ways using organophospherous
dipping. I tend to suffer from fatigue, aching muscles often accompa-
nied by blistered hands. I've a feeling I might suffer the same symptoms
if we dipped them in pure water, so perhaps it's the water I'm allergic to
- or perhaps the sheep!

A whirlwind of spained lambs

The end of October sees us sorting out gimmer lambs to go away for
winter. We went with baited breath to gather them off an allotment as
they'd been spained off their mothers straight into the trailer and straight
onto the allotment and had not seen a dog since.

There's nothing worse than trying to move and handle freshly spained
lambs. It's certainly not a job you want to be doing on the roadside with
an audience, as the best dog in the world can look a complete pillock
with a hundred lambs all wanting to run in different directions.

I remember my Dad's mate having a pink fit when someone watched
him in similar circumstances and didn't think his dog was up to much.

Our allotment is on the roadside and we spent quite a time laying our
trap with gates and hurdles and the pick-up and trailer. We arrived just
after nine and father said we could still be there at dinner time but, as
luck would have it, they ran straight in.

I think newly spained lambs are a bit like a whirlwind going round and
round and not getting very far. When eventually they do shoot off, it's
generally in the wrong direction.

Sheep wintering is becoming an increasing problem. We are lucky
enough to have a well established traditional place for ours from 1st
November to 1st April. But there is an increasing demand for wintering,
especially within the Lake District where farmers are being encouraged

not only to away winter their hoggs but yows as well.

Once we'd captured our lambs and led them home, they were to sort up, dose, tag and dip. We did not use a Rough tup last year so all our gimmer lambs are Cheviot cross Roughs. Some are half Cheviot, some three-quarter and a few seven eighths.

I tend to like them closer to the Rough, they've a bit of colour in their faces and they're bonnier and better to ken. They've also got a bit of wool to catch them by. Father prefers the tighter coated three-quarter bred ones but he's got the lambs out of them to sell and that's the sort the dealers like.

We managed to get done without falling out, but both agreed there was one very lucky lamb. It was a smaller lamb with a black patch on its eye. Can-R-Cum took a fancy to it and christened it Pugwash.

We got them safely dispatched to Cliburn for their holidays and hopefully I'll only see them once, early in the new year to dose them before April. It seems an age away but it will soon be here. I just hope I've not had to dig myself out of too many snowdrifts before then. Summer since the end of June and the back end has been so good we're surely going to have to pay at some stage.

Kirkby Mart

Tuesday nights in Kirkby Stephen have been changed for good over the last few years. When I started working for the NFU the prime lamb market was on a Monday night and was hardly worth turning up for. It clashed with Penrith, Carlisle and Kendal and the few lambs that were there were of questionable quality and dwindling fast.

The management then had the foresight to alter the market to a Tuesday late afternoon/evening and concentrate on the smaller, light, export type lamb. Of course, at the time, there were the usual comments along the lines of: "What are the silly beggars doing?" and "Do you really think farmers will turn out at night to sell their lambs?"

Well, the answer was a definite "Yes" and it has exploded into a thriving mart. I am sure many farmers' wives at the outset would be sure the old man had found himself a fancy woman in Kirkby!

There may be an upheaval in the town on a Tuesday when it looks as if it's the Land Rover and trailer centre for the North of England, but it provides useful employment for locals and the town's caterers seem to do a good trade, judging by the number of bags of chips and the like you see.

1996 saw good prices and an excellent market for the high hill farmer who often in the past found his lambs commanding the poorest of prices.

It is always the seller's ploy never to look pleased with the trade and, even this year, when no one would argue prices had been good, they all stood there doing their best to look miserable.   It's true some are better at it than others, but you rarely see a smile and I'm sure there are one or two in line for an Oscar.

The upland farmers in this part of the world are at the beginning of the livestock chain providing store and breeding animals which is fine when things are going OK as with the sheep. But, when there are problems as we all know in the beef sector, it gives the lowland farmer and finishers the chance to pass some of his losses back up the hill. The upper Eden farmer then has a problem as he has no one to pass his losses on to.

Lame Excuses

You hear horror stories about the number of Ministry inspectors in auctions and the fines if you have lame livestock deemed to be unfit to transport. I was watching all the farmers coming into the mart and thought they would have the local doctor locked up for life if they brought him up every time there was an old farmer limping or shuffling about carrying a leg.

To sell or not to sell

In 1997 Lamb prices were up and down from one week to the next at Kirkby on a Tuesday night. They are better than we ever could have hoped for at Christmas but selling is still a gamble.

Talking to one farmer who had always fed his lambs on till after New Year and was sure this year was the right year to do it again after everyone got their fingers burnt last year. At least he was sure he was right - it will be interesting to see if his nerve holds!

(I'm afraid I can give no NFU advice on this one as you could be better advised to try the 2.30 at Haydock - ask Uncle Jack).

Father, like many more, has been stuck with some lambs now the price has plummeted. He made the mistake of bringing a load home and now seems to have a weekly trip with them on a tour of Cumbrian auction marts - still, it keeps him out of mischief.

Falling prices

We all know 1998 was a bad year but just think about one or two of these facts. The mule gimmer lambs average price at Kirkby was down £34 to £44 with one local farmer's cheque for the day £17,000 down on last year.

Beef prices are at an all time low. The price of milk barely covers the cost of production, perhaps not even that if you don't send much milk. A local pig producer on being sent a brochure by his buyer realises it would cost him over £300 to buy the weight of his £40 pig back in sausages.

You go into Kirkby Auction on a Tuesday night and see any amount of bright sharp little Swaledale wethers that get nowhere near a tenner when they would have made a good £20 last year. Even father's Cheviots which are supposed to be good to sell only made £22 compared with £35 twelve months ago.

With this in mind, it's hardly surprising there was a good turn out at the NFU rally at Blackpool Football Club. The atmosphere was electric and there were people there from the length and breadth of Britain.

When I started working for the NFU nearly nine years ago, I expected a few unusual jobs but, being minder for the Minister of Agriculture was not one of them. I was there to steward but was selected on the basis (I was told) of being big and expendable. Big I don't mind, expendable I was not too keen on.

After all the farming leaders spoke, Nick Brown, the Minister, took his turn and my job was to see he got off the pitch and into the club safely. I think they were bothered about the Welshmen but it was only the press who were a nuisance.

After the speechifying there was the march through Blackpool which went off without much trouble, only a minor scuffle between our Welsh friends and the police.

You have got to admire a man with an eye for business and everyone in the local farming fraternity knows Geoff Tunstall certainly has that. He was at the march in his big van supporting the cause but, I have it on good information, it was full of leggings and waterproofs - but it didn't rain.

Hill Farmer's Lament

I heard of a farmer bemoaning the fact he started last back-end tailing his yows to give his tups a clear run at the job. He had fought on through winter and lambing time. He had done his best to produce top quality lambs and when he had finally got the cream of his crop into the ring at Kirkby Stephen, the dealers hardly looked up out of their fish and chip papers. With that as my inspiration, I have had a go at a rhyme:

The hill man's year starts in November
As he snips a bit off his yow's tail
He gives her a dip and a dose and a clip
And hopes his old tups do not fail.

He feeds them cake through his snacker
He fothers his silage and hay
With selenium and cobalt, minerals and blocks
It's pay, pay, pay, pay, pay.

There's hours of fun when lambing time comes
With its bottling, suckling and frustration
There's heads back and legs back and yows to catch
And guaranteed cold precipitation.

Soon clipping time comes
And you can safely bet
On hours of labour
And buckets of sweat.

You weigh them and feel them
And sort them with care
You get them to Kirkby
And what awaits you there?

You finally get your lambs in the ring
As Slackie eats his fish and chip tea
He glances briefly as the hammer falls
And asks - "Were they knocked down to me?"

And unfortunately as we all know too well

Another year's work
Another year's graft
And the net result?
A bigger overdraft.

Cattle

British Beef

The local NFU may not be able to sort out the beef crisis on its own but we've been doing our level best to try. On the morning of 23 October 1996, nine good men and true set sail from Darlington railway station to join the lobby of parliament in London.

The journey down was pretty uneventful apart from hearing from some of our Lincolnshire colleagues who were complaining of a poor summer with severe drought. We didn't improve their mood by telling them we'd just about had the best ever.

We were eight good men and true after the three stop tube journey from Kings Cross to Westminster, losing one along the way. Mind, we made it our business to find him again as he held the block booking rail ticket for the journey home.

We, in fact, found him outside the Meeting Hall listening to the strains of "Hoggy, Hoggy, Hoggy - Out, Out, Out" from some of our more vociferous colleagues from the south west. The singing was of poor quality but the sentiment was well meant. No one seemed to have a good word for our Minister of Agriculture with his silly hat and flasher mac.

We made a point of going past Buckingham Palace and did get a view of the Queen. It was suggested if the county chairman, Maurice Hall, was to really grab publicity for the cause, he should strip his clothes off, stick his British Beef stickers in the appropriate places and leap the barrier. His loyalty to the cause wasn't quite up to that unfortunately.

After listening to a rousing speech by Sir David Naish, we made our way to the Houses of Parliament to lobby our own MPs. We had the pleasure of saying what we thought even if we came away thinking it was water off a duck's back.

The object of the exercise, however, was to raise the profile and not the individual lobbying so we had a reasonably successful day. It will be even more successful if the man holding the £5 left in the kitty picks the right lottery numbers.

Mad cows

May 1996 - You have got to try and smile about the mad mad world of the mad cow. The member of the public putting his cheap beef into the freezer until the scare was over amused me.

So did the farmer who, on realising some sweets contained beef products, bought himself the biggest box of liquorice allsorts he could find. He did offer me one but, with his renewed taste for them, and the fact his hands were roughly the size of shovels, I didn't really get a look in.

Mad Farmers

I know we've all had a bellyful of mad cows and goodness knows what else you will be catching CJD off by now, but I've come up with my own theory.

These poor animals are catching it off the farmers. Which other section of the community would invest so much money at such risk and work so hard for such a modest return - only to be maligned by any section of the media or press who are short of a story. Look at land prices or summer grazing - I rest my case. This argument holds about as much water as the majority of others on the subject.

Mad TV

I have watched hours of Mad Cow TV and have been most impressed by the farmer quoting Rudyard Kipling's "If" - "If you can keep your head while all around are losing theirs..." To my mind the NFU has been one of the few sane voices amid mad professors, mad politicians and a clean crazy media. As I pointed out to some non-farming friends, with 58 known CJD cases out of a population of 57 million, you are more likely to die of tripping up over your willie than CJD.

After the stick I have had following this comment about catching CJD I think I'll have to start wearing my socks down the front of my pants. Mind you, anyone who's shared a rugby shower will confirm I don't consider I have much chance of catching CJD.

Double Trouble

We only have half a dozen suckler cows now but it doesn't exempt you from double-tagging. We had three calved in one week so would tag them on Saturday - what a rodeo.

Fortunately we caught the oldest and wildest first which was just as well as the whole lot, cows, calves and stirks flew about like idiots after that with heads up, tails up and sods flying several feet up into the air.

The second calf wasn't too bad to catch but bawled as if we'd cut his throat so the rest flew around even faster and the sods went higher.

The third wasn't good to catch as by this point his mother was well raised. When I caught him she was going round and round me in ever decreasing circles until we were virtually eyeball to eyeball. I wish the man from the Ministry had been there. We did get our tags in and our paperwork done and I'm glad there were only three and not 103.

Strong navels

Our local paper got in trouble for showing a picture of a bullock when writing about a prize winning heifer - it was more than just a strong navel! It's not always that easy you know. Did you watch that Eurovision Song Contest? Apparently it was a bullock that won that, even if it was bagged up and looked as if it might be taking the bull.

Wet navels

We like to think we hold the most exciting and interesting NFU meetings up here in our corner of Cumbria. Just to give you a flavour, on the issue of Trading Standards officers in auctions, one member described a run in he'd had with them over three young calves. One had a wet navel and the officer insisted it must be too young for sale. Under no consideration would he accept its navel had been sucked by one of its mates in the trailer on the way in.

The farmer got so frustrated with his inability to convince the officer of his argument he politely suggested (in reality probably most impolitely) he pull his trousers down, stand in the pen and see what happened next. The officer apparently approached him the week after and confirmed, after further investigation and, after making further enquiries, he could accept his argument. It begged the question - had he spent the whole of the last week in a calf pen without his pants on?

The Tale of Plastic Bags

This is not what you might think. It's not another moan about the dreadful summer we've had and the fact most crop has ended up wrapped in plastic but the tale of a clean crazy Charlie cross bullock.

He was born almost 30 months ago and until recently had only been handled once in his life, when he was dehorned, gelded and tagged. I don't think he's ever forgotten that though, as whenever more than one person went in the field, up would come the tail and the head and he'd fly in the opposite direction at great speed, sods flying in the air as he went.

Daughter, Jane (Can-R-Cum) was mortally terrified of him when he flew about and she christened him "Plastic Bags" as she reckoned that's what should happen to him - he should be in plastic bags in the freezer.

If left alone, his life was pretty uneventful but we did have fun with him last year when gelding and de-horning the next batch of calves, when he saw fit to go daft and buckle a gate or two.

Other than that, father's few cattle had the best of going all summer and got hay every time they bawled all winter and Plastic Bags got to be a fair size and his 30-month birthday loomed.

The nearer his birthday got the more trepidation we had, because, of course, we had to do something with him. Well, he was entered at Kirkby and the wagon was booked (we were frightened he'd bray the trailer to bits) and one Sunday afternoon, we set off to get him in.

Fortunately he had a taste for cake, not that he'd had a lot as he'd cost more in buckled gates than cake, but just enough to tempt him.

We quietly got all the cattle to the buildings and quietly got him and two other bullocks sorted off and for the first time in his life he had a roof over his head. It was very quietly, quietly - one smack over the backside with a length of alkathene pipe and he would have been at the other end of the farm.

It took some time and gentle persuasion to complete that part of the operation but it took almost as long to go through father's filing system (all big brown envelopes stuffed in a tin box) and sort out all the relevant CIDs and Passports and fill in the auction slips.

Thursday came and I dutifully turned up for my coffee to load the beasts. If you thought they were big in a field they were bigger in a confined space. After a number of laps of the hull they went in without too much trouble and I left thinking the fun was over.

The wagon blew a tyre and was stopped for some time on the Tebay/Kirkby road, pulled on to the grass verge with traffic whistling past within inches of it.

I am sure this must be un-nerving when you've spent your life relatively quietly in a field, but it wasn't Plastic Bags who was raised - it was Limmy mate - who didn't even touch the wagon door when he flew out when they finally got to the mart.

They were penned in one of those high-sided pens and he had a few goes to jump out before clearing the alleys of one or two who'd been politely asked to move and wouldn't budge.

Plastic Bags was on his best behaviour when coming into the ring and being sold, but the Limmy threw three sets of gates off their hinges before making his appearance and roaring round the ring like a wild animal.

Father was reasonably pleased with his trade the way things are - £472 - but it wouldn't have mattered because Plastic Bags was on a one way ticket and the greatest relief was getting shot of him without the loss of life or limb.

Beauty is in the eye of the beholder

I don't reckon to know much about dairy cattle. My own experience of dairying goes back to when I was a boy with milk stands and milk cans and with cows tied up all winter.

I can recollect just about being able to carry a unit and tip it into the can through the sile and put it in the old cooler that spun round with the cold water running down the outside of the can, then making out the ticket to Express Dairy at Appleby with name and address and the number of gallons.

I think the main thing that sticks in my mind is the smell; the clean disinfectant smell in the cooling house and the lovely smell of the tied in cattle, a mixture of warm cattle, sweet meadow hay and fresh bedding. The cows always seemed so contented.

At the time we went out of milk in the mid 1960s, we had part Shorthorns and Ayrshires. Since then fashion has moved on and British Friesians have come and gone and now we've got Holsteins.

I've always thought Shorthorns were pleasing to the eye and enjoy seeing them at shows and when I drive past Winton. Ayrshires and Friesians also have their good points - but Holsteins! I realise they're very efficient at producing milk and make great business sense but they're no beauties.

I had visited a dairy farmer, done our business, had my tea and was leaving when he asked me if I'd like to look at his new bull. It was a young Holstein and with great pride he showed me it and described its blood line and breeding and how many litres all its forebears produced - but what a pillock it looked. I studied it and he asked what I thought. After a while I said I could only say what my father would say - he wouldn't have it on the farm.

A year or two later, I was on the same farm and he took me to see him again and he had certainly grown out. He was like a house end with a great hump on his shoulders - what did I think of him now he asked.

"Well, he looks about fit to pull a plough" - you see them in geography books in India don't you? I understand he is actually an excellent bull and has some prolific offspring but it doesn't enhance his looks.

Milk Marketing

You may have seen in the local press not so long ago pictures of school children from Appleby promoting free milk in schools. Well, that was the official version, but the unofficial version makes much more interesting reading.

There was free milk supplied by ABN (an animal feed firm) and Express Newspapers and you had to apply to have your school on the list. This they had done at Appleby and I was recruited to try and drum up a bit of publicity. This I thought I had done quite well (with a little help from my PR lady at Skelmersdale) with local papers turning up along with Border TV.

It was all timed for 10.30am, the kids break time. We were all there like lemons at 10.30am with no milk. That was no problem, the kids would have the milk after their break at 10.45. Well 10.45 came and still no milk. I was beginning to get embarrassed, although it was no fault of my own. Fortunately we were rescued when the poor pre-school play group had their cartons of milk snaffled and we did the press call with the little kiddies milk.

So, for all the confusion, it seemed to go off all right with the pictures (ugh) getting in the papers and an item on Border News and Lookaround. So far so good.

The milk eventually arrived via a carrier from Lancashire Dairies Ltd. at 11.45, only one and a quarter hours late, so the kids would have it in their afternoon break. So all seemed OK.

The sting in the tail came when the farmer's wife who had applied for Appleby Primary School to receive the milk inspected the empty bottle her son brought home from school.

It was flavoured long life milk and, on close inspection, it had been packed in the EU for Lancashire Dairies Ltd. and, on even closer inspection, there was an "F" on the label - FRENCH MILK.

Here we were, spending time and effort promoting French Milk. It's absolutely amazing that with the milk the price it is off farm that any dairy needs to import milk. And these are the same French who will not accept our beef or even let it travel through their country - it beggars belief.

The only amusing side to it was sitting in the farmhouse kitchen getting the full blast of the farmer's wife's opinion of the French, none of which I could disagree with, when her husband pipes up - well you don't seem to mind drinking that French wine!

With appearing in the local papers and on the TV it's been a wonderful excuse for all and sundry to take the mick out of me. I'm a good hand at dishing it, so I suppose you've got to take it when it's your turn. I went into my local pub in among it all and much to the amusement of the local clientele was presented with a pint of milk!

Gone to the Dogs

Dog technology

I've written about our dogs before as they are an integral part of a sheep farmer's life, modern technology is a wonderful thing but you couldn't manage without them. They become part of your life and after a time almost part of the family.

Our oldest dog, Rap, definitely comes into that category. He's thirteen now and has been with us since he was about 18 months. Rap he was christened, I'm sure because it was short for Rapid and even at his age, he has lost none of his speed even if his stamina is not quite what it was.

Like most dogs, he loves riding on the bike as I am sure, in his mind, he equates riding on the bike with working and that's his fun. He also likes riding in the pick-up. His is the passenger seat and he's happiest with his nose about six inches off the windscreen watching the world go by.

This is all right, of course, as long as you are in on your own with him, but if there are two of us, he has to sit on the floor and he's most put out.

Mr. Rap - by Kevin Alderson, Mallerstang

I am sure he is firmly of the opinion he should sit on the seat and you should sit on the floor.

He's even more put out if you have got the trailer on and he's put in there. I guess he thinks it amounts to an insult and yaps all the way.

He's also a bit of a fool around vehicles, probably because he thinks he should be in them and I tend to let him in when I'm putting the trailer on or reversing into somewhere because you know you can't run over him if he's in with you.

Sometimes, as you can imagine, he gets a bit clarty and father plays war. He got his own back though. I was going to a rugby do at Shap Wells and was stopping at Hause Farm for the night and father was going to run me down there.

I was all dressed in my best dark suit and mother suggested he took me in the car as the pick-up would be a bit mucky.

"Serves him right," says father, "he was the last one to let that damned dog in the front of my pick-up." He took me in the pick-up and picked me up as well, so I couldn't really complain.

When both father and I are in, I tend to do the driving and father and Rap are the passengers, but they don't always get on too well. I've seen the poor dog getting wrong for sneezing after having to put up with having a smouldering fag end held under his nose.

You've not got to stroke him (the dog that is) as he just sees that as an invitation to a lot more strokes or to sit on you. It can get to be a bit of a squeeze in there if Can-R-Cum's with us as she just fits between the seats but then if we've got both dogs as well it really is fun. Father has been known to get out and get in the back!

Failed Brakes

Father came in for his coffee and announced the brakes had failed. Mother had visions of his bike being bent or his pick-up being planted in a wall, but he went on to explain his dog hadn't had any serious work for a few weeks and he was having great trouble stopping him.

Unguided missile

Rap, our thirteen-year-old sheepdog pup, the bonniest dog in the county, carries his years well and he does seem to think he's still a pup. He comes out in a morning bouncing and jumping and could really do with a three mile run behind the bike before you ask him to do something too sensible. He's even worse if you let his assistant out. Number two dog, Glen usually comes out over-excited like an unguided missile and they just try and out-do each other.

It's not too bad if you get them set off in the right direction. If not, you could be in for a crash course in bad language. Seriously though, they are gay good dogs and we've never failed to get our job done even if sometimes it isn't quite according to plan. I'm quite sure if the vet came up with a £2000 operation to knock six or seven years off Rap's age father would knock his hand off.

Rules for hill farmers' sheepdogs

I am sure you'll have seen tea towels and posters with Rules of the House and Rules of the Kitchen, so I have been amusing myself making one up for sheepdogs:

1) If the air is not blue with obscenities, you're probably running in the right direction.

2) If you do make a hash of something, don't go within one stick length of the farmer/shepherd.

3) Even if you cannot hear anything, but the farmer/shepherd is jumping up and down going red in the face waving his arms in the air, he's probably lost his voice and Rule 2) applies.

3 (a) Rule 2 will not apply if he has already thrown his stick at you in frustration.

4) Even though you've done a job 1001 times before, there's always a chance it will be different this time. If this is the case Rule 2 applies again.

5) Never bite car tyres - you could be the imminent subject of an insurance claim.

6) Don't be afraid to ride on the farm bike. You've got to get up to date just like the farmer/shepherd.

7) Don't peer through rush bushes or round whin bushes like those fancy animals on "One Man and his Dog" or you never will get your job done.

8) Never bite sheep unless encouraged to do so - a mouthful of wool and Rule 2 applies.

9) Try your best at all times. Be faithful and honest and you'll have a friend for life.

Canadian Cow Puncher

Not so long ago I spoke to our recent emigrant, Jimmy Akrigg and he was full of how wonderful Canada was, being form free but he had come across his first document to be completed for cows going to auction. He had to state their colour, brand and, if they had horns (No. 13 digit ear number). Sounds like a real cow puncher's paradise!

Jimmy Akrigg's emigration to Canada has been well documented but less well publicised has been Tom Brass'. I was talking to Tom and asked him: "What sek a spot has Jimmy gone to?" It amused me the way he described it: "The sort of place you can watch a dog run away from you for two days." A bit like Stainmore.

One man and his dog and his shovel

I often write about our farm dogs but this takes the biscuit. Rap spends half his life in the pick-up and is as good as gold but Glen, the No. 2 dog, doesn't get in so often. As it happened, circumstances dictated we had to leave him in for a while unattended. We returned to find a great heap of steaming dog muck on the passenger seat. Father went crazy - the dog got his backside that well kicked I don't think he'd wanted the toilet for at least a fortnight.

Black and White magic

No, not Alan Shearer this time either but Rap, the dog. Not only can he keep up with these go-faster Cheviots, he's also a dab hand at catching two to three-week-old lambs who get away from their mothers. I pointed this out to Rodger who agreed: "Yes, their heads just fit in his mouth."

D.O.G.

We've been scanning our sheep ready for lambing time and have most of them at home, but there are 120 down near Carlisle to do. We did the ones at home and were travelling down to Carlisle to do the rest. Wynn Parker had come to help us for the day and he was in the front of the pick-up with me. Can-R-Cum was wedged between the seats and Rap our thirteen-year-old sheepdog pup was in the passenger seat well. I warned Wynn as we set off - don't even look at that "D.O.G." He took no notice and gave him a stroke when he looked up and that was it - he was all over him all the way to Carlisle. I don't know how much petting a dog can handle but Rap can always manage another stroke.

The F Files

I thought I'd run out of inspiration and things to write about but mother has come to my rescue - she's got a new dog.

Old age got the better of Bess the last pet dog and she had to be put down and the question of another house dog came up.

My vote was to let Rap our sheepdog come into the house. He's been an honest hard worker all his life and I thought deserving of a little more comfort as he grew older.

He's bonny, extremely good natured and is almost house trained. He only pees on the kitchen table every other time he comes in. He didn't get father's vote. It takes Rap half an hour to settle himself and father only has to stir in his chair and he thinks they're off somewhere.

So mother won and she became the proud owner of a ten-week-old lurcher pup. It's a canny pup but growing at the rate of about half an inch a week and after a month could reach the back of the kitchen units.

It's a natural born thief and had its first "run in" with father when he was sat thinking it was about supper time when the pup landed into the room, laid down in front of the fire and started to devour his pie it had just lifted off the unit in the back kitchen.

He got christened Fred, after, I think, Greengrass' Alfred but there are a few more appropriate names. You could call him Trip because the rate he's growing he fills the kitchen mat now and we're forever falling over him. Piddling Pete because I'm sure he stands at the back door with his legs crossed to come in for a wet.

He blotted his copybook big style at Christmas. Mother wondered where all the egg shells were coming from until she discovered he was taking balls off the Christmas tree and chewing them up. Even worse, he managed to get himself shut in the pantry with the turkey and ate a leg off it.

He is spoilt to death and the amount he gets fed it's no wonder he's growing. We are all on short rations of rice pudding because Fred likes it. I asked mother what was for dinner one day and father replied: "Whatever that damned dog doesn't want."

Like most pups he's pretty keen on chewing things and just about everything is fair game - shoes, hats, fire brush, kindling sticks, etc. He also has a liking for paper and quite often the mail has been to piece back together to see if it was anything that mattered.

Usually, of course, it isn't and if it's a bill so much the better. He is also quite fond of newspapers but is a bit high brow, always choosing the *Daily Telegraph* before the *Daily Mail.*

He is most amusing when he's outside bounding about. He is built like a Holstein cow, all legs and ribs, and he's at that stage where he's about outgrown himself and isn't really in control of his legs. They seem to have a mind of their own. The idea eventually is he is going to catch rabbits but at his current rate of growth he'll make a good child's riding pony.

Father has an array of head gear but he is most proud of his woolly hats with the peaks like Seth wears on Emmerdale. Well, the dog got his best Seth hat and, you've got it, all it was fit for was the fire.

The builders have been on the farm putting slates back and the like following a Boxing Day blow. They were wearing gloves because they reckoned it was cold. Every now and again they took their gloves off and put them down. No prizes for guessing what happened to them.

He's pinched father's supper again. He landed into the sitting room with the paper off the bacon and the bacon was nowhere to be found. There was a plus side to this, his belly was that bad all next day he just laid about and wasn't able to get up to any mischief or do anything he shouldn't.

My kids bought him a dog selection box for Christmas and in it was a squeaky toy shaped like a snowman. He was mortally terrified of it and would disappear at the slightest squeak from it, but now he runs around driving everybody daft squeaking with both his feet and his mouth.

And, good news - he's chased his first rabbit. The rabbit went over the hill end and disappeared down his hole and the poor dog was baffled. He's not much interested in chewing shoes or pinching food when he's outside. He's too busy hunting. It's the breeding coming out - you can't beat nature.

Father read my effort about Fred, mother's dog, and told me his misdemeanours would probably fill a book. He has now eaten Geoff Tunstall's bill, much to the amusement of the farmers present; when I told him, Geoff reckoned it was a new one on him. He's also had a chew at Lesley's bill but didn't manage to totally destroy it. He is now available on hire for bill chewing.

Mother is saving silver paper for the Blue Peter Appeal and he managed to get the pot with it in on to the floor, smash the pot and chew all the silver paper.

Fred's newest claim to fame is winning a prize at Appleby Show. It certainly wasn't an obedience class or a pedigree class. No, it was a kid's photo class - so now you can see what the mutt looks like!

And more animals

The farm Moggy

One form of livestock I have not turned my thoughts to is the farmyard Moggy. Farmers usually love or hate them. On the one hand they do an excellent job keeping down vermin but on the minus side, they are far too good at breeding and have a nasty habit of leaving little sticky parcels on top of hay mews for you to stick your fingers in.

On the more serious side, cat muck on hay can cause awful problems with abortion in sheep. On the farm we have two cats, mother and daughter, and they are a murderous pair. The old cat, in particular, is an evil old bitch and I'm sure from the look in her eyes if she's not actually killing something she's working out what she's going to kill next.

She has a wide array of victims - shrews, voles, moles, mice, rats, rabbits and many of the feathered variety. When our friends do not come and take our farm bikes and pick-up trucks, they often come off the M6 to release racing pigeons. We get quite a few lost pigeons but they never last very long.

Father is no lover of cats and it just made it worse when one brought a young live rat into the house, let it off and didn't get it caught again. Ratty escaped and father was very reluctant to lay poison for it as they don't half stink if they are killed with poison. Ratty made his presence known chewing door corners and scuttering about while father tried every sort of trap he could find to no avail.

Ratty was too clever and the only thing father succeeded in catching in his traps was the dog's nose. Ratty did eventually make his final mistake and in the middle of the night got caught up amongst father's bare feet when he went for a pee. That was the final straw and smell or no smell Ratty bit the dust.

That's a while ago now and in the midst of it I told Uncle Brian the tale and he rang father and it went something like this:

Uncle Brian in his poshest voice: "Is that Mr. Sanderson speaking?"
"Yes"
"I'm the Eden Council pest control officer,"
"Huh?"

"We understand you are in need of our services,"

"Who the **** told you?"

By this time Brian had burst into fits of giggles and let the cat out of the bag - so to speak.

Big Cat Hunting in Appleby (Piggy's Pussy)

There's been a wonderful story amusing the locals in Appleby and I thought it was a shame if it couldn't be shared with the rest of the district.

H. Pigney & Son, local agricultural engineers, had the misfortune of getting a stray cat in the stores and were unable to get it out. Now, you may not think that would be too much of a problem, but of course, if cats eat as they must, they inevitably do something else and cat muck is not one of the pleasantest of things to have all over goods you are trying to sell.

But, worse than that, the damned thing kept setting off the burglar alarm and when you take pleasure out of a quiet drink at a local hostelry and you constantly have to go and reset the alarm, things get desperate. Well, desperate problems call for desperate measures, and David called on the services of his brother-in-law's desperate Alsation.

I'm not mentioning him by name because he might take offense and Les is a lot bigger than me. Well, the Alsation, as vicious as it was, didn't do much good. It didn't flush the cat out but added to the problems of hygiene by adding to the piles of....muck.

It was time to call in the professional - Appleby's own Big Game Hunter "Trapper Boots" - Gordon Shaw. Highly trained terriers were put to work and traps laid out but still the elusive moggy could not be caught. Glimpses of it were seen on the close circuit cameras but it outwitted them all. Days passed but then to much relief of all concerned, curiosity must have got the better of the cat and it ended up in a trap.

But what to do with it? The story by this time had spread far and wide so they could not give in to the temptation and do away with the troublesome puss. The RSPCA could be used but eventually a good local home was found for it.

A happy ending! - but not quite. The cat re-appeared in the yard and David Pigney was last seen chasing it up Boroughgate, past the White Hart, as fast as his legs could carry him (which is nearly as fast as seen

on TV running to the fire station).

In among all this carry on, I understand the insurance company got wind of the goings on and David received a letter along the following lines:

"Dear Sir,

Policy Conditions - Security/Hygiene

It has been brought to the attention of the company that the burglar alarm system which is part of your security arrangements has been disarmed as the result of a stray feline on your premises. The company further understand one Alsation dog has been placed in the premises during the hours of darkness for either security purposes or for locating the stray feline.

The purpose of this letter is to advise the current circumstances breach policy security and hygiene conditions because of the excreta left by the two aforesaid animals.

In view of the above circumstances, the company request you to take one of the options detailed below and be good enough to indicate to your local agent which option you have selected.

a)   Purchase a small can of Kitty Cat to lure the stray feline from its hiding place then release the Alsation dog.

b) The proprietor on returning from the Golden Ball during the hours of darkness should enter the stores, get down on hands and knees and make mouse-like noises to lure the above detailed feline from its hiding place.

c) Ring 999 and enlist the assistance of the Appleby Division of Cumbria Fire Brigade who the company understand are extremely adept at extricating local residents from tricky situations."

Little Hamster Hunting

Not so long ago I was poking fun at Fire Officer Pigney and Gordon "Boots" Shaw but I should be more careful as I was almost in need of their services soon after.

Son, James, has a hamster but from being very active it hardly stirred about at all. After the kids had gone to bed I got him out of his cage and put him on the carpet to see if he was OK.

After a bit of cleaning himself he got to walking about and then was scuttering about quite happily. He ran up the side of the gas fire and I didn't bother too much but didn't realise there was a hole in it which the hamster bolted up.

The fire is set into the old fireplace and is about eighteen inches into the wall. You can't get your hand in and the hamster was showing no signs of reappearing. Further investigation with a torch showed him right in the back peeking out - and I am sure the damned hamster was grinning at me.

We had bits of cabbage sellotaped on the end of sticks to try and tice him out, all to no avail. All efforts failed and at about 1am we retired to bed, thinking we were going to need the services of the fire brigade or our local wildlife expert.

I got up in the middle of the night to see if he had appeared but there was still no sign. I sat quite a bit more, in hope rather than expectation, as I know what a carry on there would be in the morning if the bairn's hamster was stuck in the gas fire.

As luck would have it, it appeared from under a table and I shot to the fire - blocked it up with anything I could find and set off to catch the hamster. From not moving about much it got into top gear, but eventually I got it cornered and put back in its cage and all ended up well.

I have, however, been banned from either playing with or getting out the hamster.

The Arable Farmer

Mobile Twitch

As you can imagine when dealing with some of my older customers, I am told how much better it was in the good old days. I spent an entertaining hour or two in Murton recently rolling back the years and the crack was excellent.

We were talking about a farmer from the previous generation who wouldn't let a tractor in a field with a stitching plough because they couldn't make straight stitches. It had all to be done by horse.

This rings a bell, because I've heard my father talking about my grandfather making him harrow stitches out and start again because the crows would break their legs if they tried to walk up them they were that crooked.

My man in Murton then went on to tell me about going on to a rather more modern farm where the son had been direct drilling turnips and there was an awful twitch in the rows.

When he asked him what he thought he had been playing at to make a mess like that, he explained that it must have been when his mobile rang - how times change!

Big Jeff's Wild Oats

I reckon to know a bit about sheep and cattle but happily admit my knowledge of all matters arable is pretty limited. I was visiting Southfield, near Appleby, and was perplexed at a strip of tall green stuff in the middle of the barley.

I had to ask what it was and apparently the bin with old oats in had been cleaned out on to the midden and spread with the muck. It had then struck and grown through the barley. I think they hoped no one would notice it!

The Weather

The heat is on

On the farming front, August 1997 has been much quieter after flying about in July hay timing and clipping. The way the weather's been, keeping out of the sun has been one of the hardest jobs.

We always say we shouldn't complain but at times it's been almost unbearable; being brought up and coming from Shap you're designed for the cold not the heat. I'd much rather it was 8 degrees C not 28, at least you can put another jumper on. I'll have to re-read this again in January or February when it's brass monkey weather but I doubt I'll change my mind.

Winter 1997/8 was one of the openest winters ever. No frost or snow to speak of. The start of April has been lovely. Things have even freshened up on Shap. Not a lot of grass you understand, but a change of colour of the fields to greenish and just a bit of a bite for an old yow - as long as she's still got her teeth. We started lambing on Monday the 12th and what happens? On the 13th - snow and frost.

Wet, wet, wet

You know the weather's bad when you get more farmers complaining about the wet than being hard up. Father always reckoned his idea of hell would be bad walls, dyke-broken yows and a poor dog but he is beginning to change his mind.

A wet summer followed by an even wetter winter is now favourite. He made no hay this year and is about sick of trying to feed big bales of silage to his yows when the land's hardly fit to travel on with the bike never mind his old two wheel drive David Brown tractor.

Squeeze that Seaweed

August 1998 - if you are a weather man or woman or a Met. office worker reading this, I would strongly advise you not to take a holiday in Cumbria in the near future. If you do, and any of the local peasants ask you what you do for a living, tell them you're a brain surgeon, otherwise you might be lucky to get home.

I wrote recently about John Ketley pulling his finger out - well we thought he had. He gave a wonderful haytiming forecast on Sunday, after Monday we would see the hay weather come out of the south. Well, of course, as we now know, it never happened. It got about as far as Manchester and stopped. Once again for weather purposes us Cumbrians were all in Scotland.

But the year was getting on and people were beginning to get desperate so we weren't on our own and a lot of grass got mown ready for the sun. As the week went on, the good weather always seemed to be two days away and instead of letting it spoil as it was mainly old grass to start with, we big baled and wrapped it.

In the end, every field was mown for hay and ended up in plastic wrap. It's better than a lot of bad brown hay but it bodes for a difficult winter with not really being tooled up for big bales. I am sure if father had caught up with John Ketley, he'd have strung him up by his toes, or perhaps some other dangley part of his anatomy! I don't suppose he would be on his own wanting to do that.

I took my week's holiday and the most galling part about it all is the television. As I'm sure anyone north of Birmingham doesn't really count for much and all the talk was of the heatwave in England and here we were watching the rain run down the windows.

One small consolation was the fine weather got as far as Leeds and I got to see more of the glorious final Test than I might have done. Watching Angus Fraser turn the South Africans over was quite pleasant but you couldn't really settle to it when you knew there was work to be done.

There's also an element of cost. Big baling and wrapping comes a lot dearer than a few balls of baler twine and wages for the bale leaders. Father reckoned upwards of a thousand pounds and it's not a good year for extra costs. The bale leading men were a bit put out as well as they missed out on their beer money.

The forecast for the next week wasn't good - some rain every day and what happens? Sods law again - a much better week than the one before and a much better week than forecast.

My father-in-law got the only decent hay around us at the beginning of July and I thought he had taken leave of his senses when he cut it. There was no forecast for hay but he obviously knew more than the rest of us.

I think the moral this year must be to tap the glass, squeeze your sea-weed, see if your yows are all stood a-back of the walls and then go on gut feeling. It can't be any worse than science!

Above Hause Farm and below Mike busy hay making

Can-R-Cum on the March

Above Mother, Rodger, Mike and Bob Mason
Below Hause Farm

Fred

Below, Mike, the dog and the bike

Revolting!!

Above a tricky moment with a sled full of burst bales and below, a bit of PR work in Kirkby Stephen with son James, daughter Jane & the dog.

Helping out at Rookby with Uncle Brian Cousin

Fert Spreading

Sowing Fert, June 1997

The farming year moves ever onward as it always does and as I write we have just spread our artificial manure at Shap. Popularly called fert around here, I was always amused when I worked for the NFU at Kendal as they sew till down there. They also put their cows in shippons and it was funny how many other expressions changed just by going over one hill.

Father's fert landed the same week he managed to lame his hand which I'm sure was a coincidence. He was reversing his farm bike out of the contraption it's locked up in and caught the glove, it whipped his throttle hand under the handlebars, opened the bike out and threw the whole weight of it on to his hand.

He ended up with a badly swollen hand and one thumb three times the size of the other. Being right handed it greatly restricted his movements and he was unable to drive for a while, pull up his flies, get his hand in his pocket, lift a pint glass or lift one hundredweight bags of manure.

I'm pleased to report he is recovering well and has managed to regain enough movement to be able to complete all those tasks apart from the last one. Joking apart, it was very nasty and even more galling as it wouldn't have happened if we had not been bothered by the criminal element.

Our fertiliser supplier, Geoff Atkinson from Brough, looks after lots of farms around and about and tells us we are his last customers to take it in hundredweight bags, everyone else having moved up to half tonne bags. It maybe means a bit more lifting yourself but you aren't half popular with local builders and DIY men as the bags are like gold dust.

With an old David Brown tractor and some of the hill ends we have at Shap you wouldn't want half a ton swinging around on the back of it anyway.

It's never really bothered me loading the drill by hand as you always get a decent ride on the tractor after, not like looking at a rotorspreader with a ripe. I'm reliably informed there's an EC regulation that says if you handfill a rotorspreader you've got to have at least a one mile lead.

No Peace

Two nights before we'd finally got the yows and lambs cleared off the meadows. The night before I'd sown the last of the fert. I turned up to do a bit of chain-harrowing - very relaxing - and what's been left in the middle of the barn - a great stack of wool sheets. You don't get much opportunity in this game to rest on your laurels.

Fert Spreading 1999

The farming year goes round and you carefully time when you do each and every particular job to take full advantage of the weather conditions and the state of your livestock and such like. My mother has kept a five year diary for years and it's amazing how often you do the same jobs within days of each other year after year without realising.

This being the general rule, I always know when I go from Brough to Kirkby and see Stan Scott silaging it's time to ring Geoff Atkinson and get after him to deliver our fertiliser.

Some of these men further down the hill think they're one jump ahead of us hill men, taking their first cut of silage before our grass appears to have started growing. They have their double chop/precision chop fancy foragers but we have our single chop or perhaps even single suck foragers and they're much more efficient at not even leaving the shortest blade of grass. They cut right up to the wall backs and leave less grass than on your living room carpet. As I'm sure you realise, the hill man's first cut is taken by his old yows.

The problem is then following them with the fert drill. You have a great deal of trouble seeing where you are going as there's no grass to leave a mark in. You try all sorts of tricks like turning sharp corners to turn over a bit of turf so you can see next time around. I've even seen father in front of me on the bike on top of the last wheel mark. The trick then is getting past him and splattering him with fert. I often put it on of an evening and it's amazing how much easier it is during the day when the light is better. It's also much easier when the sun shines.

Our equipment and machinery is not in its first flush of youth. It generally holds together but at one particular point I thought I'd blown the tractor up. It was making the most awful thumping noise. I stopped the engine and looked around to discover a Chinook helicopter had almost taken the cab roof off. He wasn't half low and it was only seconds before I was looking down on him as he made his way down to Tebay. It's times like this, with the trouble in Yugoslavia, when you appreciate the lads in the jets have got to practice somewhere. They never seem to bother our stock, they just catch the old farmer out now and again.

I had a frustrating time this year. The fert came and I had the whole weekend to get it on. Saturday went reasonably smoothly but it was Cup Final day so I broke off to watch it. Being a Newcastle supporter I wish I hadn't bothered but there you go - that's life.

Changing the subject, my football supporters rule has been proved to even greater effect at the end of this season - "The less you know about football, the more likely you are to support Manchester United" - and for anyone in doubt the most important goal of the 1998/9 season was scored at Brunton Park by the Carlisle United goalkeeper.

To continue with my tale. I got set off on Sunday morning and the first load went well. We use a Vicon Varispread with the waggley bit at the back, seven or eight bags at a time, depending how steep a hill you are on. I set off to spread the second load, put the spreader into gear and disaster struck - my willy waggler dropped off. The metal that held it on had corroded off a bit since and the plastic finally gave way. Unfortunately Sunday morning is not the time for this type of thing to happen as finding a replacement willy is impossible - you could say it made you feel impotent! We found something else to do, sorting and moving sheep, but it was second best when you were revved up to do a job and didn't get it done.

Haytime

Haytime machinery

With it nicely into July, I hope to be having my second week's holiday of the year, given a good growing period which we seem to be getting and then some haymaking weather. I hope to be getting my continental suntan on an old David Brown tractor. It's G registered with the G at the wrong end.

It does seem a bit outdated in 1996 but we've come a long way since I first got plonked on a grey Fergie with a single row wuffler or a Vicon Lely turner. You remember those with six large turning wheels? I can still remember being told in my early years my rowing in was like a dog peeing in the snow!

We progressed through wufflers to cock pheasants and on to haybobs and even haybobs have been improved. With all this sophisticated equipment we've got, we've managed to make well over 40 acres of hay each year with the help of the weather and a bit of luck and some willing local labour.

Being realistic, this allegedly sophisticated tackle would be lucky to cover the cost of one new farm bike - two old David Brown tractors, PZ mower and haybob, MF baler, trailer and bale carrier, all of varying vintages - you might just manage.

Of course, the vast majority of farmers may make a bit of hay but most grass is made into silage and the equipment required for this is in a different league.

As new machinery becomes more expensive and sophisticated, more farmers turn to agricultural contractors. They in turn look for increasingly modern tackle to cover more ground quicker and the value and size of some of the agricultural equipment you see travelling on the roads and working on the land takes believing.

This is the way many farming operations are going, although few workers are employed directly by the farmer, there is an increasing band of specialists who service and make their living from farming.

Machinery contractors have been mentioned, but also sheep scanners, hoof trimmers, wallers and dykers, sheep clipping gangs, relief milkers, etc. - the list just goes on. I suppose it's just part of the ever changing world we live in. Can you remember when there were no round bales or farm bikes? It's not that long since.

Haytime 1996

If you follow my ramblings, you may recall I was talking about haytiming, the equipment, weather and labour required. If you think back to mid-July we certainly got the weather - it was a hill farmer's dream come true. Just at the right time after the grass had grown and not too early to tempt you before it was ready to cut.

The only problem it was too hot. Wouldn't it be wonderful if you could make hay while it was hot and lead the bales when it was cold? It doesn't work that way though, which gets me round to what I was originally going to talk about.

At home on the farm, we've had a lot of lads out of Orton come to help lead bales and I can say without fail, they've all been excellent. All strong lads, willing workers who don't let you down - they don't get hay fever at the sight of a couple of thousand bales.

The only failing may be a tendency to develop a thirst at about 10pm but I think you can forgive that. I think the lads this year deserve a special mention because it was incredibly hot and I'm sure the temperature raises one degree for every round of bales you get nearer the barn roof. Wyn Parker, Monkey Wearmouth and Bob Mason - heroes to a man.

Hay-time 1997

The summer of 1997 saw our vintage haytime tackle just about holding together although the baler doctor was required on one occasion. Again we wouldn't have managed without our Orton based bale leaders and, although they don't come for nothing, their efforts are much appreciated especially when you hear other farmers complaining about how difficult it is to get anyone willing to lose a bit of sweat.

Our stars again were Bob Mason and Monkey Wearmouth with also thanks to Chip who proved truckers can sweat even if it was just for one night.

If you went for a pint in the George at Orton latish on it was a bit like a meeting of the bale leaders union; the local lads coming in seemed to be leading bales for half the county and if you hadn't managed to get in at least 1000 bales that night you weren't worth bothering with.

Hay-time Trivia

My mother came down to the barn with pop and refreshments for the workers and, on examining the hay, said it was that good if she was a cow she would eat it. Some wag suggested if she was a cow she would have been incinerated.

Father for some reason best known to himself impaled his hand on a tyne on the pick up reel on the baler (it really was quite nasty). As a result I got to bale a whole field of hay on my own. I think that means I progressed from being a boy to a lad - or is it the other way round. And I'm only 40.

Rodger who helps us, is multi-talented and was assisting with some building work at Orton Primary School. Much to everyone's amusement, he was mentioned in one of the kid's diaries as Bodger the Builder. Funnier than that Rodger thought it was a spelling mistake!

With my ever thinning hairstyle, I've had to start wearing a floppy hat or the sun gets to me. I even got a flap stitched on the back to keep it off the back of my neck as I was getting a real roasting. So attired I went into Fell Garage at Shap to borrow a large spanner, only to be informed they didn't serve members of the Foreign Legion.

Scientific bucket

Our meadows had been cleared of sheep, manured, harrowed and the stones picked around the wall backs when I got a bit of hassle about a mineral bucket left in the middle of the field.

I had to explain it had a scientific purpose - as soon as you couldn't see it the field was fit to mow! ADAS could easily charge you £150 for advice like that.

Well, the bucket disappeared a few weeks ago and there hasn't been a chance to mow and it is now in danger of re-appearing as the grass gets flattened by the weather.

With a bit of luck, by the time you read this my nose and arms will be peeling after a scorching week and all will be safely gathered in - John Ketley will have to pull his finger out though!

Loads of bull

After an awful year and an awful summer you have to admire a sense of humour. I was told by one man his bull was going to have a good winter. I looked puzzled and he explained any crop he'd made was only fit for the bull. Or alternatively, one man who'd managed to make over 1000 bales of hay but said there was only one decent one - the one left in the baler from last year.

Ode to Haytiming

We watched the week's forecast on Sunday
The hay weather had finally come
A bit of rain on Monday
and then we would see the sun.

Father got quite excited
He fired up his old David Brown
There was stour and smoke
But nothing broke
And soon he had all his grass down

Father got even more excited
As it rained and rained on his grass
If he'd caught John Ketley on Friday
He would happily have kicked his...behind

Father loathes making silage
He hates it with all his might
But if it wasn't for the baler and wrapper
It would all have ended up...rubbish.

Instead of being green and sweet smelling
And carefully put in the mew
It's all wrapped up in black plastic
A-back of a wall in a stew

The moral to this story is nature
Nature is always the boss
But when it's like the Government
It couldn't give a toss.

Hay-bobbing

It's amazing what your mind turns to when you're stuck on a tractor and haybob all day and the above is testament to that. As we struggled with our grass and every field cut for hay ended up being baled for silage, it struck me all the things that were wrong and I came up with this guide:

10 ways a haybobber knows he's having a bad summer
* The tractor wheels won't run dry
* The haybob wheels are always stuck up with clart
* You get your hands covered in puddle when you alter the tynes
* You think you might be doing more harm than good and would be better out of the field
* The haybob splatters you with puddle - or the back of the cab if you're posh
* You keep feeling damp spots - or seeing them on the windscreen if you've a cab
* You don't get your woolly hat swapped for a sun hat
* You don't get stripped down to your T-shirt
* You're not being followed by a cloud of dust
* After rowing in you swap your haybob for a big-bale spike instead of a trailer or bale carrier

Hay-time 1999

This summer we got half a week's decent weather and we were lucky enough to grab our hay. I managed a few day's holiday and my arms are now peeling as a result. We're also the right side of clipping which, when you set off looking at rising 800 is a relief. So, we can now relax and enjoy the rest of the summer - SOME CHANCE. There's another couple of fields we could cut; dipping those sheep will do them no harm; it's time we had some lambs away; we might get some thistles sprayed.....

With a bit of help I'm putting this book together and when we were busy baling hay my partners in crime landed unannounced to take some photos. Rodger was not keen on getting his photo taken and when asked which was his best side, announced it was his backside. Father was baling and clearly had no intention of stopping to get his photo taken but the string snapped when the balls changed, so he had no choice. "Huh," says father, "Fancy getting your photo taken with a sled full of broken bales!"

Farm Machinery

Fancy Tackle

Father got a glossy catalogue from Carr's which I am sure you would see with pictures of all their reps. and everything they sell from a screw to a tractor.

One wet June day, I was studying this book and came across this fancy new fangled piece of tackle for conditioning and wilting silage in swathes.

I had my suspicions and when I actually saw one working my suspicions were confirmed. It was a WUFFLER. It had a posh name but it was definitely a wuffler.

I spent hours in my youth on a little grey tractor with a wuffler and I only hope the new ones hold their teeth a bit better than the old girl we had. She was a bit like an old black yow (I hope this doesn't mean I have lost half the local membership!)

Camouflage

Uncle Doug Bishop at Brampton, Carlisle, takes some of our yows in for winter. The yows had been wagoned down and father and I followed on with the pick-up and trailer with a few more yows and the tups. I pulled into the field to unload and turn round and ran right over his well camouflaged rolled up chain-harrows. He thought it was most amusing as he'd forgotten where he'd left them.

It reminds me of an awful telling off father got off an old uncle who was a real stickler. He was inspecting our crop of grass which was being mown and my job was to pull the old Vicon-Lely turner out of the middle of the field once father had gone so many times round. It's a bit like looking for our bale sled - it's always in the field where we finished hay.

Mother takes great delight in winding father up and he generally falls for it but this was the best ever. Picture the scene - the old man has steam coming out of his ears looking for his stilsons. Can't find them anywhere and desperately needs them. Much to his relief mother comes to his rescue - "I know where they're at Morland....Where you left them." He wasn't really mad till then.

Good news and bad...

Father told me he had some bad news for me. He'd bought a fifteen gallon knapsack sprayer. The good news was, it fit on the back of the motorbike. What a wonderful machine...I didn't half sicken a lot of thistles in a short space of time and my back didn't ache a bit.

Farm bikes

Modern technology is starting to improve the shepherd's job. Even the most old fashioned woolly hill farmers have been converted.

What were considered toys for boys are putting ten years on a shepherd's useful working life. I know it took my mother and me 18 months to persuade the old man to buy a second-hand farm bike, another six months to get him on it and not long after that to trade up to a new one.

We've got a cake "snacker" for it now - one of these bike trailers that put cake out in heaps. Once you get the dog educated to bounce about in front of the bike it makes life a lot easier.

The sheep don't get any more sensible though. They are trying to commit hari-kari under the wheels or chasing you up the road for the tenth time that day when they should realise they only get fed once!

Dressed for the Occasion

I was invited to inspect the lack of maintenance of the drains on the railway side and was advised to come with my leggings and waterproofs. I thought it was to keep the muck out but, after being whizzed up, down and around the Helm Tunnel at great speed hanging on for grim death in the motorbike trailer, I realised it was to keep it in not out!!

Owning Up

Father threatened to do some writing to get a bit of his own back. He was going to mention how his bike coughed and farted and reeked and stunk when someone put diesel in it and how his dog got run over. Rap will stand on the back of the bike and I lost him off and the trailer went over him. Fortunately he was no worse but father's been cursing at him since to get him to lie down.

No Nepotism

I have been extolling the virtues of the bike marking scheme we have been running in conjunction with the local police. Now, don't get me wrong, I still think it's an excellent initiative but, after blowing wind off about no marked bikes being stolen, whose is the first to go? Father's. One very unhappy farmer. He was a little happier after the NFU Mutual tipped up in their usual efficient way - days after the loss. There is no nepotism here (that's a good word for a country boy).

Wrong Gear

I reckon to be able to handle most things agricultural but was beat by a new Massey tractor. I'm used to our tractors which are P-Reg and G-Reg but are David Browns with the letter on the wrong end and bear little resemblance to new modern machines. I had to move this tractor and was delighted to get it started almost immediately but could I get it into gear - could I what! I found one gear stick but not the one for the high/low/reverse box. I was later informed it was a switch on the dash - but it looked nothing like a gear lever! It would be no good to me, with that many gears, I'd always be in the wrong one.

Long Distance Tractor Driver

As we know, in this part of the world Nick Paul is a good hand at putting the world to rights and I'm sure his wife Rosemary must lose him for hours on end. I bet she got the shock of her life though when they received a parking ticket for their Case loader tractor in London. I guess either the traffic warden must have taken the number down wrong or someone's on false plates. I got someone off a year or two ago when their farm bike was supposed to be parked in Leeds City centre so I hope I can do the same here. Perhaps we should run a competition for the most novel reason for having your tractor parked in London, seeing that we might all be there in a couple of years, if current farming trends continue.

Shop local

I'm a great believer in supporting locals when I'm spending my own money and looking for goods and services which is only right as I, myself provide a local service for farmers through the NFU.

I always like to check I'm not being done but a quick look through the newspaper usually confirms Comet or Currys for instance can only provide tellies or washing machines a pound or two less than the local electrician and I know David Cleator's men will make a tidy job of installing it, will take the old one away and I know exactly where to go and play hell if it won't work.

I always thought a mobile phone would be a useful business tool but didn't fancy buying one out of the newspaper or from a big shop in Carlisle but, as soon as the said electrician started dealing in them I got one with confidence. I did go back in to be shown how to make it work rather than struggling through the instruction book.

Car dealers

I like to use the same criteria when dealing with motors and my local supplier couldn't be much more local - just across the road. Not only do you get a good local service but some good crack and the opportunity to trade insults.

I first started dealing with Roy in 1991, shortly after I moved to Appleby. I did a 17-year-old's trick after driving for 17 years. I wrote my car off after I dyked it on a bad corner. Roy assured me that if I dealt with him I would always have a vehicle whatever happened, and he's always been as good as his word.

The good thing across there is that you can speak to the boss, not some young man in a fancy suit dashing backwards and forwards to his boss and not being able to give you a straight answer. There's also always a bit of fun. Roy recently had a fresh silver Escort on the forecourt "K262NAG". I said I saw he had got a personalised registration number for his missus. Then there was the time I was getting a fresh car and he was busy explaining it had an airbag and there was a crack about having an airbag in front of me instead of one sitting beside me.

As I said, he couldn't be much handier just across the road. In fact, I am within shouting distance and one afternoon my secretary was leaning out of the window trying to get my attention when Roy smiled and said: "I'll keep her talking while you sneak around the back."

He's usually after me about the state of my car. It's a real farmer's vehicle. You wipe your feet when you get out of it. I never wash it but whenever it goes in the garage it gets washed. I think it's because he's ashamed of it.

I get grief on that subject off one of my neighbours who has nothing better to do on a Sunday morning but wash and polish his car. He thinks I am a disgrace because I won't. One Sunday it was parked next to him and he thought it was hilarious. It was filthy and because it was within hosepipe length he washed both back doors and nothing else. The car did look a bit piebald and I was looking for puddles for a day or two to get them back to the state they were in before.

Imaginary brake

We had 120 shearlings out for winter with Uncle Dougie down at Brampton and had to go down to get them in to load on the wagon to come home. These lowland men don't have dogs fit to boss turbo charged 4WD hill sheep. If I'm at home I usually do the driving and if father's in the pick-up with you it's a bit like having the handbrake on.

Well, the day before, he'd got his pick-up wheels balanced and I think a weight had gone astray or slipped just after and if you were doing between 35 and 45 mph you would have thought his old pick-up was going to disintegrate. It was to be the first time I've driven down the motorway with the pick-up and trailer when he hasn't been telling me to slow down. He's usually hanging on to his seat stamping on an imaginary brake in the passenger side.

Cracked sump

Did you hear about the NFU Insurance man who got his car stuck up a rough old farm track somewhere up Alston? The car developed a dreadful knock so, fearing the worst, he booked it into the garage. Imagine his embarrassment when his cracked sump turned out to be the boot that hadn't been shut properly.

Courting the VAT man

You're getting to see more and more double cab pick-ups about but, if you are tempted beware of the VAT man. You cannot reclaim VAT unless you can definitely prove it is used totally and wholly for business use - no trips for the newspaper or to the pub and definitely no courting!

Theft Discovery

With writing for the newspaper I often get people coming forward with interesting stories. One such was the stolen Land Rover Discovery. It was spotted leaving Wickerfield Farm at high speed, the farmer followed in hot pursuit and headed over the A66 to Bowes but couldn't catch it and the police were called out. All ended well as the vehicle was recovered - when the son came home from Appleby after dashing off for spares!

Something's got to give

I was busying explaining to one of my customers that it would cost a bit more to insure his fresh Misubishi Shogun than his old Peugeot van that had just died on him. Oh dear, he said as he turned round he'd just have to wear his clothes a bit longer. I had to point out I didn't really think that was much of an option as he had a great tear and his britches backside was hanging out.

Auction scratch

I was filling up at a local petrol station when one of my Drybeck customers called me over - could I look at his car as it had been scratched at the auction and he wanted to claim? I examined the Seat Toledo carefully and had to enquire which particular scratch he was referring to.

Family

Destroy It Yourself

I'm sure you only believe half of what I write but, before I start, I want to state that every word that follows is true. Well, I couldn't have made it up as will be revealed.

I hate DIY about the home. I'm no good at it and avoid it like the plague. I would much rather do a few extra hours myself to pay some-one else to do it, or better still let the wife do it. If there's something to do I can usually find an urgent NFU job or something father needs a hand with immediately.

I have married into a very capable family. My brothers-in-law "Our Philip" and "Our Brian" are a joiner and a builder and can both turn their hand to about anything - joinering, building, fettleing, mechanicing - you name it. Marian is also a good hand at DIY, or destroy it yourself as James calls it and is not frightened to have a go.

Well "Our Brian" has altered a bedroom for us and Marian was putting in the board to set the bed on when she caught her hand between the wall and the board and was stuck fast. Half an hour elapsed and she hadn't managed to free herself.

Fortunately she was in a bedroom at the front of the house and man-aged to get a notice in the window - "HELP, I'M STUCK." After a bit, one of the lasses up the street spotted the sign, ventured in to help but couldn't shift the board. Marian reluctantly agreed for her to ring 999 but only hoped it wasn't David Pigney who came to her rescue.

David and I take a great deal of pleasure in poking fun at each other and she knew this would play right into his hands. Well, of course, it was Sub. Officer Pigney who came charging and bounding up the stairs. It took him about five minutes to stop laughing before he could release the poor damsel in distress.

Marian told him she wished it had been someone else and David explained that was only the half of it - he had Border TV with him - and he had! They were doing a programme on Appleby. When the giggling stopped, Piggy finally got to work and released poor Marian but her rings were badly crushed and she had to go down to the doctors to have them cut off.

With ringing 999 the ambulance had now arrived from Brough and was on the doorstep so Marian got a lift down in it. They got her to the Health Centre and whoever was driving wondered is she wanted to be stretchered in. Neil Marston thought she'd rather walk in with a blanket over her head.

Well, all's well that ends well, and the swollen fingers have now recovered and we've a buckled wedding ring and a cut engagement ring. There could be an insurance claim form to fill in and it might prove to be interesting reading.

The section that asks for witnesses will make the best reading - half of Pembroke Street, Appleby Fire crew, Brough Ambulance crew, Appleby Health Centre and the viewers of Border Television. She signed the paper to allow them to use the footage and it's supposed to be on in May.

John and Sheila Raine live opposite us and Sheila never misses anything that goes on in the street - but she was away that day. I was amused when I heard John had said to her: "You spend half your life sitting looking out of that window and the only day you're wanted, you're not here!"

Piggy sold me tickets to Appleby's Fireman's dinner last year and took the mick out of me remorselessly, so goodness knows what he'll do with Marian and me this next time. I daren't not go as I am such a good hand at dishing the dirt on everyone else and I can't take the coward's way out!

Sex?

Whilst on a farm I noticed someone had written "sex" in the muck on the back of my car. I asked the farmer if it would be his kids. He said no, his son was only two and knew nothing about it and it wouldn't be his missus as she'd forgotten about it! I went into the house and she hadn't forgotten for long, she was eight months pregnant! Marian on seeing it immediately washed the back of the car. I'm not just quite sure what that means.

A Close Shave

I recently seem to have been getting comments on my close cropped hair. I used to wear it quite long as a youth but always promised myself when it did thin, I would have it short as nothing looks dafter than a long haired baldy.

Marian, cuts it for me and gave father a similar clip. It was a bit severe and his comment when his hair finally showed signs of growth was: "I thowt it was nivver gunner fog."

Stick it

Father, for reasons best known to himself, shut his little finger in the car boot and what a mess - crushed his finger, broke the bone and tore the nail off. He's made a pretty good recovery but it really feels the cold. We'd been among the sheep. He had a finger poke and a glove on and was still complaining about the cold. James, my little lad, says: "Granda why don't you stick it up your..." Granda stopped him in mid-sentence and poor James eventually explained he should stick it up his nose, which is not just quite where Granda expected to be told to stick it!

Playing Grandas

The little stories I often include are almost all true. I cannot vouch for this one but it tickled my sense of fun. A little lad is staying with his grandma on the farm when she loses him. She eventually finds him cursing and swearing and kicking his bike. She's in the midst of ticking him off when he says: "Don't worry Grandma. I'm only playing Grandas."

The dog

I take my kids with me on a Sunday to the farm. Father and I were having great trouble moving and sorting some yows and lambs when my mother asked James, my seven-year-old, what his Dad and Granda were doing. "Just shouting at the dog" was his reply.

Dodgy Keeper

One of the highlights of January 1999 was a trip with the two kids and Uncle Brian Cousin from Rookby to St. James' Park to see Newcastle United play Liverpool in the Coca Cola cup quarter final.

We enjoyed the evening out but not the result - Newcastle went down 2-0. The best part of the night was the second half when Liverpool defended the Gallowgate End where we were sat. It's where they make all the noise and they started chanting: "Dodgy Keeper, Dodgy Keeper" at David James, Liverpool's goalkeeper.

It doesn't look much in print but chanted in a strong Geordie accent was quite amusing - especially as with even a scant knowledge of football you know Newcastle fans aren't really in a position to accuse anyone of having a dodgy keeper.

This tickled son James and for a week or two everything was dodgy. This wasn't too bad until his mother got a new frock to go to a local dinner dance. What did he think of Mummy's new outfit - "Dodgy Dress."

We nearly didn't come home with Uncle Brian. He went for a pee at half time and hadn't landed back after 25 minutes and we were just starting to panic.

Anyway he did find us but he'd got himself in the wrong tier too low down. He told a steward he was looking for a big man in a white woolly hat and he soon saw me right at the back. I could just hear the announcement: "Can Mr. Sanderson please report to club office to pick up his Uncle Brian."

Sour Beer

Poor old father isn't as young as he was and last year we got too good a start clipping and his back was bothering him. Mother's cure all is a frothy bath but father is a three baths a year man, whether he needs one or not (apparently they wash away your natural body oils and should be avoided).

The back must have been bad as he had his bath. Rodger and I were after him next day, "How mucky was the water then?" Father reckoned it was clean enough to drink. I looked at Rog and he pulled a face as if he had a mouthful of sour beer!

Holidays

Dad and Mam usually get a weekend away between lambing/marking out and before clipping/haytime. I get left in charge and it is usually the time any old yow thinking of dying actually gets round to it or some temperamental piece of old machinery finally decides to give up the ghost.

This time I had a lamb run over on the fell road and I must admit the motorist concerned was good enough to come and own up. He said he thought he had winded it. I went back to the scene with him and it had a broken back leg, a broken back and he had hit it that hard he had let its

gut out - Winded! As he stroked its head and apologised to it I resisted the temptation to tell him what I really thought and explained I would have to take it home and shoot it, to put it out of its misery.

On these weekends I get the use of the company vehicle - a red Toyota pick-up. As often happens they picked Appleby New Fair week to go away. The biggest problem is getting through Appleby without picking up a load of youths thinking you're one of them and wanting a lift back up to Fair Hill.

Holiday 1998

I had a week away in Ireland with the family but not before a hectic day or two. We went on the Saturday but the Thursday before is Appleby Show and, being treasurer it causes a lot of work, not just for me but perhaps more importantly, for Marian. It's not just the show itself but the build up and then all the sorting out afterwards.

During the aftermath of the show we fell heir to a loaf of bread shown by Mrs. Linda Pigney which we ended up with when clearing out the industrial tent. It was really quite good and the kids took a fancy to it.

As you can imagine we had quite a rush getting packed up for Saturday morning but we made it to Stranraer to catch the Seacat to Belfast at dinner time.

Radio Cumbria had been at the show and we hadn't been able to listen to it so Jane taped it and we listened to it on the road and heard Mrs. Pigney and her mam being interviewed.

It was Saturday the 15 August and we set off across Northern Ireland bound for County Donegal in Eire which is the bit that wraps itself around the west of Northern Ireland.

We planned our route and the most direct path was through Omagh. We saw a lot of Army helicopters and Land Rovers but thought little of it until we heard on the radio just five or ten miles short of Omagh that the bomb had gone off. If we had been an hour and a half ahead of ourselves we could have been right among it. Makes you think.

Anyway we arrived safely and spent a comfortable first night and spent the first morning eating Mrs. Pigney's toasted bread watching the rain run down the windows.

Our cottage had an open fire and we were supplied with peat bricquettes which were a bit slow burning so the first thing we bought on holiday was a bag of coal - tells you something about the summer.

If anyone thinks the Irish have stolen our summer I can assure you they haven't. There were chewed up fields all over the place and wrapped big bales tucked away in corners everywhere. Every big bale we saw was stood on its end and I couldn't work out why. I thought it might be so they didn't roll away but they were like that in flat fields as well - any ideas?

There was some excellent farms inland but where we were on the west coast they all seemed to be trying to farm eight or ten acres of rocks, rushes and seeves. They all have nice new excellently appointed white bungalows with very posh gates and drives all no doubt courtesy of some European scheme.

At the end of each bungalow, almost without fail is a tatty old building with a Massey 35 or 135 parked up beside it. In Donegal they must have the highest number of tractors per head of population anywhere.

Planning permission is a joke. These bungalows just seem to sprout up everywhere and they just stick signs and notices up as they see fit. We even saw a couple of wind farms on top of some Lake District type mountains, all of which you wouldn't see here.

They do have another advantage over us - diesel at 45p a litre, it's neck end of 70p here. The exchange rate helps. James' eyes nearly popped out of his head when he took his English tenner to the post office and got £11 Irish punts. He thought all his Christmases had come at once.

I was calling the weather bad but we did get one good day on the beach which was a very cosmopolitan affair. We were playing cricket and on one side some youngsters were hurling (that's a real man's game) and on the other side two Americans were practising baseball (girlie rounders).

We got our week put in and I'm glad to say our journey home was a bit less eventful. I was reading through my mail when I got home and had a bill from H. Pigney & Son - the cheeky beggars had sent a bill for "a show quality loaf of bread."

Holiday 1999

The timing of our family summer holiday is very tricky. We daren't take it too soon or it's bound to fall in the first fine week when we're hay timing at Hause Farm and that would never do.

The second Thursday in August is Appleby Show and as I'm the treasurer we can't miss that so we usually plump for the week after. It's a bit of a rush with the show on the Thursday, banked up on Friday, then packed up and away on Saturday.

The 1999 show went reasonably smoothly with the only real bone of contention being some kiddies' pony entries. Someone suggest to me the only good place for a horse is on the back of a stamp (get it - straight from the glue factory). I couldn't go along with that, of course.

We got banked up and had a pretty successful day. At this point, I must own up and admit, Marian does the vast majority of the work. I am just there to get told off.

Saturday morning came and we were off bright and early on the road to Holyhead to sail across to Dublin. Everything went according to plan and we caught the fast ferry to Dublin which was very pleasant. The journey was pretty uneventful until we came to unload. It was a double decker car deck and we were on the top deck, one off the front. It worked like decks in a livestock trailer and once the bottom deck emptied the front of the top deck lowered. The car in front of us couldn't have had his brakes on properly as, when the deck came down he rolled forward and would have dropped off the edge but managed to get anchored up. My heart was in my mouth watching from behind so I bet he had striped underwear.

We travelled the ninety miles down the coast from Dublin and found our cottage we had booked from the brochure. We knew it was new and it was just like its picture. What we didn't know was there were another fifty of the damned things! I like to get away from people on my holidays not be among hundreds of them!

The holiday complex backed onto a resort which was like a down market Morecambe. I don't like to sound snobbish, but we went into the town for our suppers on the first night and got some fish and chips from an outfit called Jackpots. If I told you it was opposite a run down night club, was full of machines and a bingo hall and its name was in three foot high letters with the tops of the "J" and "T" snapped off you will know what I mean.

All you had to do though, was turn the other way and you got into the type of Ireland you expect - Slow, Quiet and Easy. The only time we had problems was when we visited a castle which had a couple of coach loads of Germans in and they rammed about like a division of Panzer tanks pushing you out of their way - with no excuse me or by your leave.

We found some lovely clean, near deserted beaches and had some nice days. I often write about Can-R-Cum who is now a teenager. Here we were flouncing about doing our best to look like a "Spice Girl". When we got to the beach she tore off in her little trousers and crop top and announced she was going to dig a hole. She went from thirteen coming on eighteen to thirteen coming on eight in a flash and eventually landed back soaked to the skin and covered in sand - some Spice Girl.

I kept an eye out for Paddy the farmer and they were busy harvesting when we were there - my favourite moment was watching him coming up a hill leading big round bales with not a rope in sight and seeing three or four bales rolling back down the hill. It was very droughty and was apparently the driest part of Ireland. Anywhere where there was livestock you struggled to see what they were living off.

Fuelling up there was a pleasure paying 53p for diesel instead of 74 or 75p here. It made about a tenner a tankful difference which wouldn't have half added up over a year - it's that level playing field again.

We put in a pleasant week and the only drama left was almost missing the ferry home. The roads weren't too bad back to Dublin, but every time they narrowed we caught up with a tractor or a really slow wagon. We even met the Irish version of the Tour de France and had to wait in the roadside as they went past. Even so, we had time to take a detour in Dublin and were the last car on the ferry. We did keep off the top deck though.

Christmas

Christmas for me doesn't really start until dinner time on Christmas Eve. Tina and I have the office party at The Royal Oak with the help of one or two of my insurance associates from Penrith.

After finishing our lunch, it's up home for coffee and Christmas cake, drag Marian down off the ceiling as the kids have usually driven her up the curtains long before then.

I then get them out of her hair and do my now traditional parcel delivering round to uncles and aunties and both sets of parents. The only break in the proceeding is in my role as treasurer of Appleby Show on the door of their domino drive. We had a poor turn out this year basically because it was such a bad night and perhaps because we had no heating last year.

I don't think I've ever been out on as bad a night as Christmas Eve 1998. There's one thing for sure, if it had been snow, we wouldn't have set off over Orton Scar.

Christmas Day started early - about quarter past five as I remember - and I apparently missed the start. Santa seemed to do quite well. He came up with a silver bike with ten gears instead of a red bike with fifteen gears for James which appeared to be just as good, other than that, James, who is a keen Newcastle United supporter had a black and white Christmas.

Santa was also good enough to bring Jane a typewriter/word processor which I am using at this minute. When writing I'm always extremely careful with my spellings and grammer (or is it grammar?) as my mother is a stickler for such things.

She bought me a dictionary of Cumbrian dialect for Christmas as she was sure I was spelling yows and spaining wrong! I also got a couple of bottles of the hard stuff and a jumper which looked enormous but fitted like a glove - I suppose that should tell me something.

After present opening the rest of the day is a bit of a gastronomic delight - lunch at home, tea with mother-out-law and then supper with mother at Hause Farm.

All went well at home. Christine Johnson from Castle Bank's turkey was prepared to perfection by Marian. Her mother's Christmas cake and mince pies were up to their usual standard but the problem came at Hause Farm - No Electric.

The Aga is oil fired so they'd got their dinners, eventually though, as it does have an electric pump and the temperature was well down. In an old farmhouse with small windows on a dull day there was very little light even with an array of candles and a couple of paraffin lamps.

No television of course and it was also impossible to read or see instructions so my little niece up for the week had a very quiet day as did everyone else; a bit like a Victorian Christmas.

Father wasn't at all pleased and even the thought of the electric he was saving didn't cheer him. I left after a few hours with stinging eyes from the fumes and there were complaints of sore heads and eyes next morning that had nothing to do with red wine or the odd wee dram.

And lo, Boxing Day came to pass, and still the damned electric was off. I went to bullock for father in the morning and the first job was to fight on and re-light all the candles and lamps. As you can imagine by now the Victorian Christmas was wearing a bit thin.

Coffee time arrived and then from the east came three wise men in a Norweb Land Rover and power was restored. All was then revealed and they all saw what they'd really got for Christmas, how many fag ends and empty glasses were laid about and how much wax a dozen candles make!

Townies

I know our friends in the towns look down their noses at us peasants who make our living off the land, especially the more unsophisticated ones of us in the hills. They want to take a look at themselves, as I often think they are more like sheep.

They spend a large part of their day following each other about like sheep, bumper to bumper, usually in some fancy turbo charged flying machine when, for the speed they can manage to go at, a bog-standard Ford Fiesta would be more than adequate.

I avoid it like the plague, but walking on city streets is worse than being herded like cattle. Even on holiday they cannot give up their obsession of following each other about. We watch them on the Coast-to-Coast walk at Shap following each other, strung out in a line like ducks. They don't enjoy the scenery or discuss what's going on around them, just trudge away looking at the heels of the person in front. We know this for sure, because the last one in the line never sees if a gate was shut or open and invariably leaves it open.

I hate to admit it but my sister, Anne, is a cross-bred townie. She moved from the splendour of Shap to work in Newcastle for the Civil Service. I must own up and say I don't complain when she queues at St. James Park to get us tickets to watch Newcastle United.

Living in Newcastle and working for the Civil Service is bad enough, but just imagine what father thinks when she brings the boyfriend home in the middle of summer and he watches pop music on television while everyone else is sweating outside in the hayfield. For a hairy old hill farmer that's bad enough, but what do you think he made of this?

She had a birthday barbecue and a lot of her friends came across. We had a right good do, but we couldn't understand why all these lads were stood outside the loo. At first, father thought it might be something to do with the way he was barbecuing the sausages with a blow torch but, on further investigation, they were all waiting to have a pee, AND, waiting for the cistern to fill up each time - takes some believing!

She's a keen photographer and we were busy examining pictures taken of the kids on the farm, and father and I were discussing how much grass there'd been that summer and which fields in the background had just been haytimed. She said she couldn't believe us, but of course, she doesn't understand that farming and sheep are the most important things in the world!

Dialect

When I write these bits I can baffle my computer. It has a spell-checker on it which is marvellous as it keeps my mother off my back because of my pathetic spelling but it doesn't recognise Cumbrian. Mother does though and bought me a dictionary of dialect for Christmas to keep me right as she was sure I wasn't spelling yow and spaining correctly.

It's really very good and makes you think how you use words but it doesn't attempt the ones father uses when things aren't going according to plan. I spent my school days at Heversham being called "Baddle" as I once said someone was badly when they were ill. They'd never heard that expression. But I was right - it's in the book.

Bureaucracy

Objectionable

We've heard all about the Euro funding that's available under Objective 5B and I've got into trouble before for calling it Objectionable 5B as I've never worked out the location of the cheque book. I heard the best one recently though - Objective 5 Bugger All.

A little later on I was speaking to Nancy Tweddle who is on for Cumbria Farm Link and I told her I reckoned this European money that's supposed to be about should be called Objectionable 5b as it was a waste of time and no-one could get their hands on it. What a telling off she gave me, so I promised to give her a mention, but she said not to tell you she had the cheque book.

Daft Dipping Forms

Talk about confusion and bureaucracy gone daft - if you'd have rung the Environment Agency at Penrith at the start you would have been sent a dip form. They then thought the job wasn't going on fast enough and sent everyone one. Nationally they finally got into gear and mailed everyone another form, not the same form of course, just to keep you on the hop. So that was three forms. Then, if you deal with Youngs they sent you one for good measure with an offer to fill it in. But, the last time I saw Cliff Main he was heading out of the auction at Kirkby in a cloud of dust and later declined to fill in father's form. The only good thing I can say about the whole carry on from my point of view is, it should only to be done once - famous last words!

I don't even like to think about it but I guess you'll have the big brown IACS envelope by now - if I have got through the dip disposal forms, I'm at your disposal for the IACS forms. Please forgive me if I swear at you.

A Teaser

Can you solve this problem? I was sent on a visit to Stoneriggs. With the average hill farmer's income officially quoted at £2,400, who can

make well in excess of ten times that income out of sheep with no investment?

Which man with lambs so difficult to finish can make 70p out of every
lamb whatever the market conditions?

You've got it - the MLC man. Arthur has many phrases to describe
them but "bunch of bandits" was the most repeatable.

Transport rules

I'd like to get the rule makers together who came up with the rules for
watering and feeding stock before you transport them and ask them when
they thought the sheep had drunk and eaten enough.

When they said enough, throw them on the bottom deck and load the
lambs on the top deck and see if they changed their minds after an hour
or two when the reconstituted watering and feeding they had approved
was running through on top of them.

Just before you load young kids into the car for a long journey, do you
give them a big bottle of pop or send them for a pee? Enough said!

Cattle competition

Did you know the new Cattle Movement Service at Workington are running a competition? The winner is the farmer to receive his passport
applications in the most envelopes. I have heard of three and up to six
but the leader in the clubhouse is Geoff Taylor at Swathburn with nine.
And the prize - a waste paper bin!

Customs and Excise dippers

It's not very often you get one up on the Customs and Excise men but
one of our locals did. He was working on a site where they were dipping
everything in sight. Could they dip his old Mazda pick-up? He gave
them the keys and they landed back after a while as mad as hell. Why
didn't he tell them it was petrol - well they hadn't asked!

Leicesteritis

I am writing this on 4 February, a date I have been looking forward to all
January, as it is the closing date for claim forms for sheep premium and

hill subsidy.

The Ministry always have the knack of asking the same questions in a different way each year just to confuse everyone. This year they seem to have hit the jackpot as I've had more calls for assistance than any other year.

The best question on the form is something like: "What is the date of the last entry in your Flock Record Book?" Now that raises a few blank stares - what's a flock record? The usual reply was that green book you got off me two years ago and have written nothing in since. What it is, is quite simply a running total of the breeding sheep you own with additions and subtractions for purchases, sales, deaths, etc. You have to detail the causes of death and in some completed books I've seen this can raise a smile.

Natural causes is the main excuse but there are plenty of others - "brain damaged" was one of my favourites - it didn't specify if that was the sheep or the farmer!

"No idea" is probably most truthful but my favourite I couldn't read right off. The farmer explained his scratchy hand-writing wasn't some fancy new disease but "Leicesteritis"! In the recent storms I heard of a farmer who knew 99 ways a Leicester could die but he'd just found a 100th - a gap had rushed on one.

MAFF Carlisle

Anyone who knows me will tell you I'm no great lover of the Ministry of Agriculture. It was with great interest I undertook a visit to their offices at Carlisle with colleagues of mine within the county. We saw floor after floor of offices and row after row of desks and heap after heap of files. We did learn that there are two sides to every story and they have their problems as well as us.

It was quite pleasing to hear they agree some of the rules they have to impose are as silly as we think they are. Their attitude was extremely helpful but you get the impression their over-riding fear is of the European auditors looking over their shoulders.

We saw the staff who work there issuing CIDs and passports and paying HLCA claims. I found out once you get your HLCA letter saying they'll pay on X number of sheep, the cheque is on its way which helped me solve a problem the next day.

I could also help the man who rang up complaining MAFF had lost his file. I could assure him they hadn't because I had seen it on the top of one of the many heaps I'd seen the day before.

To the uninitiated in agricultural matters, farmers are able to claim support payments on certain livestock and crops but can only claim on a certain amount per acre.

The support payments keep farmers in the countryside and without them much of the land would be "ranched" with the knock on effects being run down farms and buildings, broken walls and hedges.

The acreage system means the farmer declares the amount of land they farm so the Ministry can check they are not claiming too much. A relatively straightforward process you would think - not when you are dealing with the Ministry of Agriculture!

IACS or ISSAC's as it is sometimes affectionately called, stands for Integrated Control and Administrative System (also quoted in some parts as Infinitely Awkward and Completely Stupid) and comes just at the time of year when the farmers in this area are least able to manage it.

Tempers can be short enough at lambing time at the best of times. The form itself comes with an explanatory booklet which defies belief, last year running to some 77 pages - the most practical advice would be to ignore the book and read the form.

The information actually required is details of fields, their Ordnance Survey numbers and area. Three years ago this caused sheer panic in the agricultural community and queues outside Ordnance Survey centres.

At that time the Ministry didn't seem to care that the majority of higher ground had not been re-mapped since before 1970 and no acceptable field numbers or areas were available and re-mapping was paid for at the expense of the hill farmers.

Once they have the information on their computer in subsequent years the task is to check, sign and return their computer printout of this information - a piece of cake!

Not so, the proliferation of mistakes the second year was awful and once you sign at the bottom, their mistakes become your mistakes, and your livelihood could and probably will depend on it - one mistake could mean the difference between profit and loss.

Last year I completed over 150 IACS forms and on about the 149th the farmer suggested it was all a plot by the NFU to get members to pay their subscriptions or get non-members to join.

I asked if he would let me know just which NFU man had thought up the idea as I would quite gladly take the nipper to him and I was sure I'd find a volunteer or two to hold him down.

I had one particular customer who was in a dreadful twine about the whole thing and cheered up when I told him completion of the form was voluntary.

I went on to advice him if he didn't fill it in the Ministry man wouldn't send him any more little brown envelopes and he quickly changed his attitude - "Let's have the bloody thing filled in then!"

Intelligence Test

I have helped a lot of folk with their sheep forms this time round and am convinced it's not because of the difficulty of filling them in, but fear of the Ministry. I am also looking to find someone who failed the MAFF intelligence test, who put the form in the envelope the wrong way round and posted it back to themselves. I can't find anyone who will own up.

If you have not had a letter from the Ministry querying details on your IACS application, I think you could well feel left out. They are in the process of writing to almost everyone questioning the smallest discrepancy when they compare the details you've given with their maps. The fact their maps are out of date and in any event don't cover half of our upland area doesn't seem to matter. The two important points are if you get one of these letters, don't panic and secondly, if you want a hand to sort it out just ask me as I'm getting to be a better map reader than the keenest of walker or hiker. Mind you, if you see me walking around with a map tied around my neck, you will know I have finally gone crackers.

I've just recovered from this year's bout of IACS attack. The question for sheep farmers on common land amused me. I was fair itching to answer the question 'When do you gather your sheep?' with "On a fine day when the bike will start and the dog will run." I did think better of it though as officials and humour rarely go together.

Mike's Manifesto

I'm no lover of politicians of any hue and think we should really have a "politically incorrect party". With tongue in cheek, I put to you its manifesto:

* Eating beef on the bone to be legal - as long as the bone is British.
* Pasteurised milk to be made illegal - antibodies for all.
* Recognition for a hereto ignored ethnic minority - The True Countryman
* Equal rights for men - sorry dear - ouch!
* Outward signs of homosexuality banned - punishable with a little orange rubber ring.
* Tax free diesel for NFU members - white diesel prices for the rest!

The term "pig" to be banned in Tamworth - pigs will now be called Bacon on Legs

* Introduction of a Tourist Tax - to be shortly followed by tolls on footpaths
* The Government & Ministry of Agriculture to be accountable for their own mistakes - a farmer led committee to oversee
* Kevin Keegan to be re-instated as Newcastle United manager with the return of Beardsley, Ginola, Asprilla, Ferdinand and Beresford
* Death penalty recalled - for sheep rustling and child abuse

Europe

Our fortunes are more and more linked with what goes on in Europe and there is a constant stream of European news of one sort or another. 1998 saw the so called lifting of the beef ban but it was more the first step in an awful long process.

The same year we had the World Cup in France, so of course, we have been getting into trouble with our football hooligans.

It always makes me think of the Duke of Wellington at the Battle of Waterloo when he said he didn't know what the enemy made of his troops but they certainly frightened the life out of him.

When our football "supporters" get on to the continent, they have a habit of chanting: "If it wasn't for us you would be Krauts." They've got a point which is fetching me round to my point - the central European currency.

The arguments have been raging about whose head or flag should be on it. To my mind it's quite simple.

Churchill's head on one side and a Lancaster Bomber on the other, because if it hadn't been for the great man, we would have had the central European currency 50 years ago, only it would have been called the

Deutsch Mark and there would have been a funny little fellow with a tash with his picture on it.

We, as farmers, know all too well there's been a constant stream of European directives many, it seems, with the sole intention of frustrating and bankrupting us. We've had everything from a ground water directive to illegalise your dipping facilities to rules banning the export of whole yows.

It's amazing from how far and wide the market is affected. Who would have thought the number of bottles of vodka Boris Yeltsin sups would knacker the Kirkby cull yow trade? But it certainly has.

There is one thing agriculture should be thankful for from a European point of view. As long as we can get what the rest of Euro agriculture gets, they have a stronger voice as there's more of them, hence more votes and therefore their politicians take more notice.

National Farmers Union

Rodent

I was amused by Peter Stott writing in the NW Farmer when he said his computer's spell checker kept wanting to alter Rodney Bacon to "rodent". It's obviously a highly intelligent piece of equipment. Can-R-Cum got a little hand held calculator type spell checker at Christmas and it also wanted to turn Rodney into rodent. We tried each other's names and poor Marian suffered. It wanted to call her a "Martian".

Three Wise Men?

We've had an NFU carol service this year and in my Christmas newsletter I appealed for three wise men and a virgin. It's a pretty serious slur on the local membership, but I got no volunteers under either heading. Gordon Deighton was keen but as he and Hazel are starting a family again after a number of years, he thought he failed under both categories!

Have your cake and eat it

Working for the NFU, I spend a lot of my time collecting money, be it in the form of insurance premiums or subscriptions.

I do try to do it as painlessly as possible but always try to bear in mind one of my father's favourite tales about the old farmer who was being pestered by a particularly persistent rep.

He wasn't making much progress with the old lad who eventually explained how his farm finances worked.

"At the end of the month all my bills get put in a hat and I pull them out one by one and pay them until there's no money left - and if you don't get off my back, yours will not even go in the hat."

Geld?

I am sometimes asked by the staff in the insurance office at Penrith to translate farming jargon. One young lass was in on her own at dinner time and was stuck and gave me a ring. Could I explain what a geld cow was? I advised her I hoped she was geld and explained why. What was a cast cow? I told her she wasn't cast yet and explained why. She then read out the problem the bull had (ventral deviation of the penis) which was why these cows were geld and I was almost lost for words to explain why they were geld - almost, but not quite...

Cake Advice

I was given a particularly good insight into the talents required to be a successful NFU man by my predecessor Jim Nicholson.

Jim explained how one afternoon he called on one farmer, conducted his business and had a very pleasant tea provided by the farmer's wife.

He then moved on to the neighbouring farm and was again offered his tea which he politely refused, explaining he'd already had his tea next door.

"What's wrong with my cakes?" the farmer's wife demanded. The golden rule is of course...never fall out with the farmer's wife and eat up all her cakes.

I have a keen member who is always after me to try and sign up his near neighbour who is a keen non-member. I was there

one day, doing my best. The crack was good, but I wasn't making much progress. At this point I threatened to come back next time with his neighbour and pick him up by his ankles and empty his pockets. His wife told me the last thing we would find would be money but I said a bit of string and pocket knife would be a start. I left with no subscription but an invitation to go back for my tea whenever I wanted.

Crash course

I'm always on the look out for new members to recruit and use all sorts of reasons to try and twist their arms. Offer to fill in Ministry forms, write letters for them and such like, but my most unusual method was to put my car into the prospective member's dyke at high speed.

As you can imagine, he wasn't overly impressed to start with, but I owned up and got him a decent settlement for the damage I'd caused and now he's one of the converted. I don't think I'd like to recommend this method on a regular basis!

Mistaken Identity

Here's a story out of the NFU insurance office at Penrith. One of the lasses (well almost a lass) took a phone call from a firm called "Ellis and Buckle Loss Adjusters". She didn't quite catch the name and transferred the call and said she thought she'd got a pop group on the phone - Alice Buckle and the Drifters.

Tax dodge

I was recently consulting my accountant (cousin Paul), and discussing ways of reducing my tax liability. At this stage, I should really extol the virtues of an NFU Mutual Pension Plan or tell you about the excellent performance of the NFU Mutual ISA but, between us we came up with a much more efficient way to avoid tax - Take a Farm!

Naughty Frilly Undies

From time to time, usually when trying to convert the non-believers, you come across the old chesnut - "You DO know what NFU really stands for don't you?" (As in No Fing Use). I thought I could come up with an alternative - how about New Farmers Union - it certainly worked for New Labour. Not For Uglies. Or perhaps more aptly Nasty Fat Uglies. What about Naughty Frilly Undies (that's something you didn't know about Ben Gill) or, more loyally, Now For Urgency and No-nonsense Flatout Undertaking. Alternatively Nice Friendly & Unique or No Further Urbanism. Thinking of our continental cousins - No Foreign Upstarts or Nauseating French Usurpers.

Station Master Bob

Me, Uncle Brian and another ten good men and true went down to London to the NFU's "Keep Britain Farming Rally." We left Darlington at 9.30am to arrive in London at precisely 12.11pm, bang on time. Our return journey was also to the minute leaving London at 6pm to arrive back in Darlington at 8.22pm. We couldn't praise BR or whoever they are now too highly.

My only gripe would be the ticket telephone number I rang which after the seventh attempt put an answering machine which told me to ring after 9.30am when it was already 10.30am. I then went up and saw "Station Master Bob" at Appleby and couldn't have received a more helpful or courteous welcome and got me fixed up with just what I wanted - modern telecommunication technology leaves a lot to be desired.

Once in London we had to shoot through the underground system to get to Central Hall for our meeting. We did get split up once but Uncle Brian made sure he didn't get lost this time. He wore his own distinctive hat - it was a Trilby that would have been a credit to Arfer Daley - we were expecting him to start selling Dodgy Gear at any moment.

Countryside Rally

Before the day of the Countryside Rally I wasn't sure I would be able to go with sheep-scanning commitments and a winter weather forecast so travelled down by car rather than on an organised coach party.

Sunday 1 March 1999 started early knocking three inches of snow off the car windscreen at 5.30am. Early progress was slow over Orton Scar and even slower getting stuck on the fell trying to get to High Woodend at Tebay to pick up George Horn. We eventually hit the M6 then the M1 passing numerous "Countryside Coaches" on the way.

Once we got to London we had a cunning plan. We would get off the end of the motorway, find the first tube station, park up and tube ourselves into central London. All went well initially until we located the tube station, parked the car, bought the correct ticket only to find the line was shut all weekend - some plan!

All was not lost. There was a replacement bus service and we got into London and onto the tube at Baker Street. After a minor detour we finally got on the right train and headed for the Embankment.

The tube was absolutely jam-packed, full of marchers with rich accents from every corner of the country. Talk was of horses, grain prices and were we lost? But mainly how could anyone do this every day.

We passed stations crammed with people wanting to get on but couldn't because there was no room. The system virtually ground to a halt. We got to our destination and finally came up for air and the scene that greeted us was barely believable.

There were people with banners and placards as far as the eye could see. I have been in big football crowds before but nothing to hold a light to this. There was no crush or push like a match but just a quiet shuffle, the good humour and wit were outstanding, the feeling of togetherness was unbelievable.

There was a complete cross section from the hoity-toity horsey set to the rabbit and ferret men, fresh faced YFC members to the Major/Colonel types of the grouse moors, the obvious farmers with big hands and weathered faces to pretty young veterinary students, they were all in it together.

The good humour spread to the banners being carried. Here's some of the ones that caught my eye: "Eat British Lamb - 500,001 foxes cannot be wrong" "Let them roam in the Dome" "Ban sex - you have a one in 97,000 chance of producing a politician" and "The only Fosters that makes sense comes in a can".

The peasants were revolting but they were also good humoured, decent, well-behaved, tidy and I was mighty proud to be there and be one of them.

I've never hunted in my life but was greatly impressed by the Countryside Rally in London in 1997. I've read a lot in the press and spoken to some who attended and they were a credit to those who live and work in the countryside. Their behaviour and the state they left Hyde Park in was a revelation to those in attendance (especially compared with the gay march the week before).

I've never been on the floor of the stock market or in some rough inner city area and would not claim to know anything about them but neither would I dream of telling them how to go about their business. Unfortunately some urban dwellers don't seem to have the same attitude, fox hunting today goodness knows what next.

There are many pros and cons to the hunting question but to my mind it is man harnessing nature to control the fox and whatever our townie friends say they DO take lambs. Perhaps not in great quantities but when you consider our local fell packs kill in excess of 100 foxes a year they soon would.

I know there is a lot of tradition involved and a hunt is a social event but I fail to see what is wrong with that. Too many old traditions have fallen by the wayside and everything modern is certainly not always an improvement.

I firmly believe you have to live in the real animal world to appreciate the arguments and the amount of drivel and pure ignorance talked by some "antis" has to be heard to be believed.

Real life is nothing like Walt Disney and if you'd seen worried lambs personally, you might appreciate this. I don't know about you but I'm not sure what to make of an administration that wants to ban a legitimate country pastime but is happy to leave the way open to allow 16-year-old schoolboys to be legally at the mercy of adult homosexuals!

It's a Queer Do!

We were all a little bit disappointed with the coverage of the Blackpool Rally, but there were further developments. On the Sunday, the Min. of Ag. was "outed" - guess who was shown on Sky News talking to him as he left the football pitch - yes, yours truly! I'm with the leading Cumbrian NFU Delegate on this one; I'll stand shoulder to shoulder with him if he wants to defend British Agriculture - but not in front of him.

City folk

I went to the NFU AGM at the London Hilton for the first time this year and was most impressed by it all. I expected to come away thinking it was a waste of money but if you are an organisation that takes itself seriously and you want to draw media attention and influence people it's no good having two mouldy sandwiches and tea in polystyrene cups at Knutsford Service Station.

We walked down Park Lane to get to the meeting and it seems to be all car showrooms - BMWs, Mercedes, Range Rovers and the like with nothing under £50,000, of course. There was a Toyota showroom but there were no second-hand Hi-Lux pick-ups. There was also a newspaper stand and half the papers were written in Arabic which probably explains quite a lot.

Being in London is all a bit of an eye-opener. I've been to London to NFU rallys at the Houses of Parliament and to Twickenham and Wembley but never spent any time in the city centre watching the world go by.

It appears to be full of important people rushing around doing important things, all carrying a brief case and a mobile phone. You wonder how they managed before mobile phones were invented.

There again, are they real? and have they just got their bait in the leather-bound combination locked briefcases and have they just been sent out to run someone an errand?

Tina's Anniversary

Time rolls on and I've been with the NFU in Appleby for nearly a decade and it seems like a long time but, spare a thought for Tina. July 1999 was her 20th anniversary of starting work for the NFU. Either me and Jim before me must have been good to work for or she must like farmers. There again, she might just be soft in the head - I know which theory I would go for!

It's worth repeating the conversation heard in the local agricultural engineers between two farmers - "I've just been in the NFU office and if that lass' skirt gets any shorter she needn't bother wearing it."

Hands On

I've been heavily involved in helping organise the rebels against the proposed Pennine Bridleway and I'm sure you'll have seen some of the publicity we've got.

Well, Radio Cumbria. wanted to do a piece so I roped in rebel number one, Arthur from Bank End. This extremely attractive young lady came from Carlisle to do the piece. She was tall, thin and blond. We found Arthur clipping out cattle and he was muck over head.

He said he'd have to go and wash his hands but we couldn't just work out why he needed clean hands for a radio interview... unless he had something else in mind.

Show Time

Parkers Paradise

Although not strictly a farming subject, I spent the first Sunday in August parking cars at Lowther for the Horse Driving Trials. No, I haven't found another occupation. Penrith Rugby Club charge the show to do the parking and players and helpers supply their labour to help club funds. It works well.

It really is a mammoth task and if I had a pound for every car I'd parked I doubt I'd be writing this now. If only I had a pound for everyone who wanted to park under a tree I still would be pretty well off.

There were numerous reasons for desperately needing to be under a tree. It was usually because they had a dog in the car, but there were also ferrets, babies and even one with his granny who was going to stop in the vehicle. Mind, what he'd brought her for if she wasn't going to get out beats me!

There were all manner of folk, from the upper echelons in their Range Rovers to the lads out of the North East in a battered old Ford Escort van with a box of ferrets and a terrier.

One of these lads got out of his van, stretched his back, looked at the thousands of cars on view and said in a broad Geordie accent: "By, you could do a lot of car radios in an afternoon here!"

I was amused by the owner of a Land Rover Discovery who as soon as he pulled up, pulled his wheel clamp out of the boot and secured his pride and joy - I rather cheekily said to him he needn't have bothered with that as Discoveries were a bit like backsides here, everybody has got one.

There was a disabled parking area close to the entrance gate and it's surprising how large a percentage of people considered themselves disabled, at least for parking purposes!

I'm afraid I am not very politically correct and I was also surprised at the number of couples and families who were driven by the lady - not that I've anything against lady drivers, of course, I wouldn't dare.

Dominoes

I enjoy a game of dominoes and was playing at The Gate at Appleby. We were playing against the farmer who lives opposite and had quite an entertaining evening. He was meant to be leaving in decent time to look over his lambing shed.

At going home time he was showing no signs of moving so we loaded him in the back of my partner's Toyota pick-up and led him home. We ended up among his sheep giving him a hand for our troubles. We also got a thrashing at dominoes so next time we'll load him up before we start playing.

YFC Dominos

My main aim is to amuse so I'll report on our latest clash with the local YFC. They challenged us to dominoes, pool and darts at the local pub and the outcome was an honourable draw after a very entertaining evening. I roped father into playing 5s and 3s. We both reckon to be able to play but were on the verge of being acutely embarrassed by James Brownrigg who could play a bit and Heather Wildman who reckoned she couldn't play at all. Lady Luck came to our rescue.

The highlight of the evening was, after much studying and giggling, Heather played 4-2. Father carefully explained if she'd have played it on the other end she'd have scored 4 instead of none. "Oh, I'll do that then" she said. "Oh no you won't" replied father and put it back on the other end. These youngsters don't realise what a serious game dominoes is! It's our turn to challenge them now so we're busy thinking of something we might beat them at.

We've thrown our weight out and challenged the local YFCs to a rounders match - there's no fools like old fools!

Gurning

Father scored a great victory and won the gurning competition at The George Hotel, Orton, at the Lunesdale Hunt Do. I have it on good authority it wasn't his official entry that took the prize, it was third, but the face he pulled when he picked up a poor hand of dominoes. Now, if they thought that was gurning they want to see him standing a poor trade with his lambs on a Tuesday night at Kirkby!!

Given out "LBW"

We all know times are hard and things are tight and anyone collecting money in farming circles is going to have a struggle but I heard a good one when one farmer told me he was dealing with his bill on an LBW basis. I couldn't quite see the tie-up with cricket until he explained - "Let the Buggers Wait".

Photo Opportunity

My kids are keen on putting entries into Appleby Show and for a week or two before they were busy making scones, doing handwriting and this year taking photos. They spent a day on the farm when we were making big bales taking photos of sheepdogs that wouldn't sit still or cats looking in the wrong direction, trying to get the perfect entry.

Cheviots of Fire

We were discussing the lack of classes for Cheviots at local shows, considering how popular they are among the local farmers. I suggested, considering their speed, perhaps Cheviot racing would be a better bet. "Would that be something like Cheviots of Fire," quipped Maurice Hall.

Not bales but bails

On a rare evening off among the clipping and haytiming, I ended up at Water-Yat Bottom with my family and we had a game of cricket. Some time later, the bails had gone missing. On my next trip up Mallerstang I was instructed I had to go and look for them. One lovely sunny afternoon, I was apparently wandering aimlessly about when two of my Asby farmers' wives pulled off the road. "So, this is what you get up to then." I told them my tale but I am sure they thought I was putting the day in just sunning myself.

Appleby Fair, 1996

In Appleby we've just nicely got over Fair Week. You will have seen the lovely pictures of the black and white horses in the Eden in the centre of town being washed and the old characters on the hill bartering for horses.

Lovely! They don't show the mass of bottles, cans, chip papers etc. that are to clear up every morning by the council workers before the whole charade goes through its next 24 hour cycle.

No one explains the travellers' aversion to using the few portaloos that are provided and the mess on neighbouring land. It's a bit like being under siege for a week.

Those farmers in the close vicinity and not directly involved have to make their silage in the weeks before the Fair and then batten down the hatches for what is becoming Fair fortnight. If it increases at its present rate it will soon be Fair month.

It's not just farmers around Appleby who are adversely affected. Graziers of Cote Moor on the Sedbergh road have had their common invaded by up to 50 motor drawn caravans and 25 horse drawn vans at a time with, at its height, 70 horses grazing where they do not have a right.

This goes on to a greater or lesser extent for over three weeks with minimal toilet facilities and also no organised supply of water. Nearby troughs are utilised with consequent damage to troughs, gates and walls.

How would you like someone camping in your back garth or garden unannounced with vehicles, caravan, three goats, five dogs and two horses?

Appleby Fair, 1997

June has come and gone and with it the Appleby Horse Fair with all its associated attractions and problems. I'm sure all us in and around Appleby will be pleased with the way the powers that be have put their foot down and kept the fair to its true dates instead of letting it start two weeks or so earlier and slowly build up.

Not so pleased will be all those on the roads leading to Appleby as the "jungle telegraph" came into operation and the travellers realised they were not going to be allowed on to Fair Hill early.

As a result they set up camp anywhere and everywhere where there was a park or a wide road verge. I know I travelled to Scotch Corner the week before the official start and there were caravans and horses parked up at every turn.

We can only hope those in charge stick to their guns and our travelling friends realise they shouldn't set off to Appleby quite so soon and next year everyone should have an easier ride.

The town was busy again this year as it is bound to be but to me it didn't just seem quite as busy as it had been and it appeared to break up a bit earlier. I talked to quite a few of them who reckoned they hadn't had as good a do this year. The horse job is on the floor (it's not just sheep, beef and milk). I was told by one dealer more vehicles would have changed hands this year than horses.

Countryside Matters

Embarrassed

I was co-erced into sponsoring the local F.W.A.G. farm walk so I went along to have a look at the walling, dyking and wildlife.

As with most farm walks there had been a tidy up and all the old implements, pallets, etc. had been cleared to the back of the yard so folk could park.

I had taken my kids with me and James said in his biggest voice: "This yard isn't as big as Chris Sowerby's". (Chris being the local scrapman with his yard next to the school). They really can drop you in it.

I also got my arm twisted to go on a farm walk at Broxty for Kaber Village Hall. James went with me but Can-R-Cum was badly and didn't want to come but everybody wanted to know why Can-R-Cum hadn't cum.

Just somewhere pretty

I remember being taught in physics at school, for every action there is an equal and opposite reaction (or something like that - it's a long time since) and anyone fiddling about with the environment should give some very serious thought to knock on effects.

The beautiful surroundings are in no small part due to the country people who have lived and worked in this area for the past hundreds of years.

If Eden district council or the Lake District planning board existed two or three hundred years ago would anyone have got permission to put up the dry stone walls or field houses that are now so highly thought of?

Almost as bad, if not worse, are those who move into a country village and want to change everything after two minutes, or who want to make sure theirs is the last property that's developed. It always seems to be offcomers who are complaining about things that might help the local community, a quarry or a bypass.

I suppose that the point is a lot don't see the countryside as a working environment, just somewhere pretty.

Right to roam

There is a lot of work to do before the "right to roam" legislation actually becomes law but, in reality the public treat a lot of commons and fells as if they have the right now. You only have to look at the Lake District to see that, but even at Shap we have people pulling off the M6 to exercise their dogs and have a picnic and locals as well having a walk and walking their dogs.

99 per cent of these folk are perfectly OK, pick up their litter and are no problem. I know father encourages one particular man who walks his old sheepdog each morning to keep the sheep in front of him as he is gathering them up to feed and saving him a job. Father was quite amazed when he had a crack with him and asked him how old his "old dog" was. It was about four or five and could hardly go whereas our sheepdog "pup" is eleven-years-young. Just goes to show hard work and a good cursing every now and again does you a power of good - I'll have to keep repeating that to myself.

Touroids

I've got into trouble before when writing about walkers, but I'm afraid I am no great lover of tourists of any ilk. They invariably slow the progress of the workers, with boots and rucksacks, mountain bikes or even sightseeing cars.

I am aware of the arguments about them putting money into the local economy which I fully appreciate and I suppose I should be thankful I don't have to live and work in the Lake District. It would, of course, be different if I was making my living off them - some of my farming clients have diversified and do a nice side-line in tourism.

I was amused by one of my farming clients who was pulled up by the police on his tractor on the A66 for not pulling over with a mile or so long queue behind him on a bank holiday. He hadn't impressed the constable when he explained it was alright because he was working and all those behind him were on holiday with nothing better to do.

My problem is, that for one week a year, to my horror, I'm like the rest of them and become a "touroid" (a touroid is a term for a tourist as they are loosely related to haemorrhoids).

I spent a week in Devon on the south coast and now appreciate our corner of Cumbria even more. There are far too many folk down there. It's far too hot and there are far, far, too many cars. I promise never to get too aggravated ever again if I get stuck behind two or three old biddies in Appleby or Kirkby Stephen - we don't know how lucky we are.

My kids had a marvellous time. Where we stayed had an array of brochures for all the local attractions and our week was planned within half an hour of landing.

The farming near the coast was a bit foreign with not a sheep in sight. They were farming grain and ponies. To keep the kids amused when we were trailing about, they got a sweetie if they could spot a sheep, farm bike or Toyota pick-up like Granda's - they didn't lessen the sweetie bag very quickly.

We did have a ride on Dartmoor where we found plenty of sheep. Far too many of course according to our green friends. I was quite surprised how many Roughs there were. Our week was well planned and we ended up on the beach, on a steam train, the zoo and a butterfly sanctuary, but one leaflet we didn't follow up was a Hedgehog Haven at Prickly Ball Farm (honest!)

I did get a bit of local crack and on the subject of tourists. They reckon they all come down to Devon for the week with a clean shirt and a £5

note with the intention of changing neither. This may be true but I would have struggled to find much to spend my money on where there would have been change out of a fiver.

It's frothy man

We'd just got the tups and few hoggs in and got a nice start to clip and it was pouring down. We were working away and thought someone had beaten us to it as there looked to be some freshly clipped sheep down the fell next to the motorway.

After looking more carefully we could see it was rubbish blowing about. It looked like sheets of white plastic. It was only when we got a look at the gutters running off the motorway at home we realised exactly what it was.

Enquiries to Cumbria Constabulary revealed a tanker had been broken down the day before and leaked some "harmless" detergent and the first heavy rain had frothed it up. All the gutters and drains coming off the motorway were three foot deep in froth. It makes you wonder how much harmful stuff comes off the motorway along with the rubber, oil and salt we all know about.

This appeared to be a harmless incident, but I think it highlights the way farmers appear to be victimised and are a soft target for the environmental agencies. There are numerous bodies and sets of eyes watching slurry pits and silage stores and they are currently going to town on sheep dipping facilities.

Whilst no one could defend anyone who knowingly pollutes, the motorway is there pumping diesel, rubber and heavy metals into water courses every time it rains.

If we've had a dry spell the next heavy rain that comes turns all the becks and streams running away from the motorway into rainbows, that's what the oil slick on top of the water looks like and livestock will drink the foulest looking water rather than drink out of the beck.

We've had a mild winter this last year, but in a normal year thousands and thousands of tons of salt are spread onto the motorway and every single grain is going to end up in the local water courses. It's the only place it can go.

But do the highway authority have to catch their effluent and dispose of it in a reasonable environmentally friendly manner? No... it's much easier for the Environment Agency to pick on individual farmers, threaten them under some European Ground Water directive with a £1,500 license to dispose of their dip when there has never been a recent instance of groundwater pollution in Cumbria.

I know this sounds just like a moan, but it's symptomatic of agriculture's current ills - more and more regulations and rules to comply with which means more and more costs when there is less and less profit (if any) to fund them out of.

There are also different bodies pulling in different directions. The Environment Agency, I'm sure, would like to see an end to the dipping of sheep, but what of animal welfare? Woe betide you if your flock gets scab and falls into a poor state and the RSPCA get after you.

Walkers

I am often having a go at walkers, but remember a particular day when the boot was on the other foot. It was 3 January and I was in a car going to play rugby at Cockermouth.

I hope there's no-one from Cockermouth reading this, but playing there in the middle of winter was no joke. I am sure the town sewerage system drained through the pitch. It was always up to six inches deep in puddle. The showers at the time, if we were lucky, dripped luke warm water, and the play was never anything less than physical.

We were approaching Keswick and the rain was being blown horizontal by a gale force wind when we saw a group of walkers.

"Look at those idiots" said someone. It was then pointed out perhaps they weren't so daft when you considered what we were about to go through. At least they had waterproofs on and looked as if they were heading for the safe haven of the nearest pub!

Walls and dykes

If you have a ride out in the country in this area, you cannot fail to notice the hundreds and thousands of miles of drystone walls. From the super straight newly constructed walls alongside such as the A66 improvement to the old meandering walls on the lower ground which have been walled and re-walled over the centuries.

The workmanship and skill is to be admired especially when you get higher up and see allotment walls going up seemingly vertical hills and mountains. From the farmer's point of view, the most important bit is the walled and re-walled bit because walls do not look after themselves and need constant maintenance.

The farmer could do this himself but, in these days of ever increasing productivity, he has less and less time and the job usually gets passed on to contractors. Our green environmental government paid grants to all farmers who participated in dyking and walling which encouraged the farmer to employ these contractors, keeping the countryside attractive and tidy and employing local labour.

Unfortunately, this is no longer the case and not just anyone can apply, only those in certain areas or with particularly attractive schemes, so the run of the mill farmer is left on his own with his walls.

It always seemed such a sensible way for the government to spend its money because it has two benefits - one environmental and the second to the rural community which is under ever increasing pressure. The way modern day thinking goes, perhaps we should be setting up a gay or lesbian walling group. I am sure we could attract European money or a grant from some daft London council. I must admit the walling men I know in the district aren't that way given as far as I know.

Wildlife

I wrote a couple of months ago having a bit of a go at environmentalists and do-gooders and have had quite a bit of feed back. Tell them: "The killers are protected," was one farmer's reaction. His views were the spiralling numbers of badgers was bound to be pressurising ground nesting birds and the hawks that ten years ago you watched in wonder, are now an everyday sight and must similarly be pressurising the population of smaller birds.

Like badgers, there are an awful lot more of them about and, it stands to reason, they've got to live off something and they certainly don't all live off carrion.

I read in an article it was all the farmer's fault that small bird numbers were dwindling because of the use of pesticides. I don't know if this is true further down country but there's certainly no pesticides used in the hills and fells in this corner of Cumbria.

As with most of these arguments, there's more to it than meets the eye and the first most obvious cause shouldn't always be blamed as something else apparently unconnected can have a knock on effect.

Tiddles the cat is getting a bad press at present for killing birds which is most unusual and goes against my argument about everything cuddly being protected.

I am often told by the agricultural community on the subject of environmental bodies and schemes - do they not realise if the farmer hadn't created and looked after all the things they are so desperate to save, they wouldn't be here to save in the first place!

"Where have all the lapwings gone?" Did you see this one day seminar advertised? I would have thought the answer was pretty simple - down the buzzard's throat.

Bird Calendar

I was amused to consult my diary one day and see an appointment had been booked in with a gentleman from the RSPB - Royal Society for the Protection of Birds. It sounds a bit posh and a bit well organised consulting my diary so I must own up and admit my diary consists of a large calendar I write appointments on.

I didn't know quite what to expect, as I am no great lover of greenies, environmentalists and the like. The lad who turned up was a decent sort and we got on reasonably well - the fact he had a sense of humour helped - so did the fact he was six foot seven or eight.

What he was after, was my willingness to circulate a calendar they are producing to promote their campaign for wading birds in the North Pennines. Every month they had a pretty picture and what the farmer could do in that month to help oyster catchers, curlews, peewits and the like.

I can remember in January you hadn't to overgraze and in May you hadn't got to chain harrow nests on the ground. What a good idea I told him. Which month is set aside to shoot badgers and buzzards and give the peewits a real chance?

He couldn't agree with me, of course, but did have some sympathy with my point of view that some environmentalist types have tunnel vision for their particular area to the exception of other areas and an apparent lack of ability to see the full picture and the knock on effects just looking at one particular aspect can have.

A wonderful example is hawks. Once upon a time, not too long ago, you would have stopped and watched one if you were lucky enough to see one, but now they are common place. You even see buzzards on the roadside fighting with the crows and magpies over a rabbit hit by a car. He couldn't argue with me when I got on my pet subject of overgrazing on heather fells. If the heather was regenerated and the grouse came back, it would be wonderful for the moneyed man with the shotgun but disastrous for his wading birds.

He had a sample calendar that had been produced in the south which had plenty of pretty pictures even if you weren't too keen on the message, so hopefully by December, I'll be able to let all NFU members have a northern version free of charge.

Farmers often get a bad press on environmental grounds but I would like it noted, on the records, all spring operations came to a halt on my father-in-law's farm when a blackbird nested in the cab of one tractor and a wren in the radiator of another.

Health Matters

A Pain in the Neck - and elsewhere

I don't see why only half the local population should be amused by my misfortune, so I thought I might as well share it with the rest. Can anyone explain why, with most illnesses and ailments you get a reasonable amount of sympathy, but when it's anything to do with your bottom everyone thinks it's hilarious.

I've had a boil up my backside and was doing a very passable impersonation of John Wayne walking down Dodge City after seven hard days in the saddle - sitting down was a tricky manoeuvre and getting into the car was worse. Some things were worse than that, but I won't go into detail, as I know the gentile nature of some readers.

I'd been to the doctors twice, which to anyone who knows me, shows how bad it was. On the second visit he sent me to Carlisle Infirmary to get the offending item drained. Little did I, or the doctor realise, all I was short of was a swift ride to Carlisle with the wife driving through every pothole and over every cats' eye! I got out of the car in the Infirmary car park and my waters had broken, either that or I had lost control of my workings below.

Within minutes the relief overtook me - wonderful! We still went ahead and saw the consultant "Mack the Knife". It eventually dawned on me what he wanted to do - take his knife and wreak havoc in my nether regions. I had been offered an alternative operation privately the day before in H. Pigney & Sons, something to do with bending over a desk and a Stanley knife and, to be honest, it seemed by far the better choice.

With lambing time only a day or two away, the thought of being laid up for a fortnight could not really be contemplated, so I had to politely explain my position and refuse his kind offer to put me through all kinds of agony. I stand a chance of the condition re-occurring but, touch wood, so far so good.

I was given antibiotics to take which meant I couldn't have a pint and, as anyone who knows me knows, I do like a pint. The course of pills was for a week and it was no problem - it wouldn't have mattered if it had been for a fortnight or a month - so you know how unpleasant it was!

The lady vet

Farmers on the whole are a pretty sexist lot. The fact that in many cases it's the farmer's wife who "wears the trousers" doesn't come into it when considering the outside world.

Female vets have only been considered fit to geld cats, polish dogs' teeth or look after your hamster or goldfish. They were only fit on farms for decorative purposes - that is, of course, until Lesley moved to Kirkby Stephen.

Father has a saying about the "Regiment of Royal Standbacks" and it's quite true. Handling wild stirks is a bit like playing rugby - the harder you get stuck in the less you get hurt.

Lesley obviously subscribes to this philosophy and although her femininity is not in question, in a loose shop with a heap of bullocks (or potential bullocks) she's better than most men.

I first came across her one Saturday morning when she turned up late to geld and dehorn some strong stirks. Father gave her a rousting for being late but she told him off for getting her at the weekend when she was on duty on her own.

He explained he could only get his staff at the weekend and she said she would have got the stirks in for him - AND I'M SURE SHE WOULD HAVE TOO - even if they were nine-months-old and had never been handled in their lives!

We got on dehorning them and she got those long handled clippers on one particularly strong bull calf and couldn't manage to shut them.

Father was at that end of the crush and got hold of the end of one handle in an attempt to assist but wasn't sure about the other end as it was nestling in the groin area. He was wavering when he was told in no uncertain terms to get a hold and get the job done.

Just as amusing was, after the fun and games were finished outside, we went into the house for a wash down and a cup of coffee. Mother's cat had got its front legs nipped and was in a bad way so, while Lesley waited for her coffee, she had a look at the cat and said given time it would heal - and so it did.

You should have heard the Old Man's language when the next vet's bill landed. Called out to dehorn and geld cattle - fair enough - but the fee for the cat inspection didn't go down well at all! When he calmed himself down and got himself to the vet's, it turned out to be a dear cup of coffee.

I haven't sought Lesley's permission to write this, so I hope she's not lurking behind a wall with the nippers!

Lesley's Number One

One Saturday morning Father was booked in for brucellosis and tuberculosis testing and there were four stirks to geld. We weren't sure who was going to do the job for us but we were pleased it was Lesley because the crack's always good.

We had our "handling facilities" all prepared. In true hill farmer tradition a couple of racks, a few gates an old cattle crush and plenty of binder twine/baler twine/Michael/farmer's friend/Hause Farm hinges - call it what you like.

Lesley decided she would geld the stirks first while she was clean! In any case there were only four to do. We were pretty well staffed as we had Rodger in attendance and we got the first bull in no problem at all. It was too good a start and we had a real chase to get the second one in the crush.

Rodger was quite philosophical saying he'd take more getting in than that if he was to "do" and Lesley said she was glad there were only four to do. She proceeded to do her job but couldn't get the stirk to stop bleeding. We waited and waited and waited and eventually I said I was glad we only had four to do and she told me to stop pinching her lines.

While fighting on getting the next beast in it caught me with a pretty good kick. Lesley asked me where it had caught me. She was standing there with a blade in one hand and a pair of fancy looking nippers in the other. I refused to tell her. The last bullock "to be" put up a marvellous fight and we had to physically drag him into the crush. Rodger had him by the head and I had him by the tail and an eight to nine-month-old stirk takes a bit of pulling.

Well, that was one half of the job done but we'd succeeded in raising the cows and we struggled to make anything of them. We eventually had to lessen our pen to make anything of the old cows. That's one thing about temporary structures, you can move them. Lesley dived in to help.

I was dragging one rack and her the other. "We've got our legs knotted together" she said as we got the racks tangled up - "Sounds more fun than testing."

We eventually got our job done and Lesley reckoned she'd had a disappointing morning - Father hadn't got knocked over into the clart, and what was most unusual, he hadn't even got his hat knocked off.

Blood and batter

I can get myself into some scrapes while on farms, but the best one was when I arrived early for an appointment and they were just completing a caesarean on a cow.

The lady vet was on with the final lot of stitching when the cow started bouncing about like something not right. It appeared the anaesthetic was wearing off too soon.

Anyway, things went from bad to worse so I tried to make myself useful and piled in and did my best to hold the cow down while she finished the job.

She managed to complete the operation and here I was covered in blood and batter which didn't really bother me till I took notice of the farmer. He was hanging on to the halter wrapped around a posting and was as clean as a pin. And my best jacket...

Pearls of Wisdom

Have you heard Arthur Slack's Pearl of Wisdom? In these trouble times, why is farming getting more like sex? Because, the more you think about it, the harder it gets! Or, alternatively, why don't farmers need Viagra? Because they're always hard up! I was also told another good one about Bill Clinton, Tony Blair and an old yow with its head caught in a wire fence, but you'd better ask me - I daren't print it!

A nasty dose of orf

We've had a nasty dose of orf among our lambs which has needed much spray, orfoids and the like. I went into the vets at Kirkby and asked for some long acting penicillin for father. There was a lot of giggling while they guessed what he needed injecting for but I eventually explained it was for his lambs and, if I wanted a bottle of anything for him it would probably be calcium. There's nothing worse than orfy lambs but we persevered, and finally got the better of it but I spent a few weeks with purple fingernails - I suppose purple fingernails are quite good for an NFU man's "street cred" (much better than a mobile phone!)

Small animals

For reasons far too convoluted to go into, my little girl's pet cat had to be injected at the vets. Picture me in the small animals queue with the old ladies with their dogs and kids with cats and hamsters. Now being from a farming background where bangs on the head and lead injections are the order of the day, just imagine how I felt when someone I knew came in! The only plus out of the whole situation was it got put on father's bill.

Jippy Tummies

We seem to live in a world of food scares, the latest being the supposed link between red meat and cancer of the colon.

It's not quite that simple when you take a closer look. As I think everyone knows, too much of anything is bad for you and that is all they are really saying when you get down to it. But of course that sort of view does not grab headlines. Bad news does grab column inches and TV coverage but when you consider in the last 20 years red meat consumption has dropped by 25% and cancer of the colon has increased by 20% the slant on it hardly seems justified. I'm not worried in any case as, when I eat beef or lamb, it is always brown!

The other thing is how much do you believe these scientist type people as there are plenty of items considered bad for you once upon a time which now, in moderation, are good for you - beer and potatoes spring immediately to mind.

I don't think the powers that be are doing the population as a whole any favours with over protecting them - pasteurisation, homogenisation and sterilisation all have their place but humans need some germs in their systems.

A nice example was an on farm NFU meeting where there was a cream tea provided. No one knew what just wasn't quite right but the NFU office type men all suffered with jippy tummies for a day or two and the old farmers never batted an eyelid. They were used to raw milk and the odd bug or two.

Would it be a good idea for the population as a whole to have to eat a sheep muck sandwich a week? The taste might not be too good but think of the antibodies!

The Poor Old Man

Whenever father is asked what he thinks about my writings his usual reply is: "When he can't think of anyone else to take the mick out of, he takes the mick out of me." So, I suppose I must close by thanking him for his patience at being the butt of my humour and also thanks to all the others I have poked fun at. It is all meant in good fun and I hope taken in the spirit it is intended.